Setting Boundaries with Your Adult Children

ALLISON BOTTKE

HARVEST HOUSE PUBLISHERS

EUGENE, OREGON

This book is not intended to take the place of sound professional advice offered by a family counselor or therapist. Neither the author nor the publisher assumes any liability for possible adverse consequences as a result of the information contained herein.

For privacy reasons, some names in *Setting Boundaries with Your Adult Children* have been changed.

Cover design by Garborg Design Works, Minneapolis, Minnesota

SETTING BOUNDARIES WITH YOUR ADULT CHILDREN
Copyright © 2008 by Allison Gappa Bottke
Published by Harvest House Publishers
Eugene, Oregon 97402
www.harvesthousepublishers.com

Library of Congress Cataloging-in-Publication Data
  Bottke, Allison.
  Setting boundaries with your adult children / Allison Bottke.
    p. cm.
  ISBN 978-0-7369-2135-0

  1. Parents—Religious life. 2. Family—Religious aspects—Christianity. 3. Parent and adult child—Religious aspects—Christianity. 4. Adult children—Family relationships. 5. Intergenerational relations—Religious aspects—Christianity. 6. Empty nesters—Family relationships. I. Title.
  BV4529.B675 2008
  248.8'45—dc22

                                                                  2007019417

Printed in the United States of America

10 11 12 13 14 15 16 / VP-SK / 17 16 15 14 13 12

To every parent or grandparent with an aching heart.

"With God all things are possible."
Matthew 19:26

Contents

Acknowledgments

The longer I live and the longer I write, the more people I have to thank for making every book come to life. God has blessed me greatly with family, friends, co-workers, and an amazing publishing team whose encouragement, support, and love make all the difference in the world. You know who you are—thank you from the depths of my heart. Yet without readers, it would all be for naught. Therefore, I wish to extend a heartfelt thank you to readers. It is for you this book was written. *Setting Boundaries with Your Adult Children* was a tough book to write—a book that was decades in both the living and the writing. It is my prayer that within its pages you will find hope and healing.

It is also my prayer to share true short stories from parents and grandparents who have been victorious in breaking free from the cycle of enabling. If you've never heard of our true short-story compilation books *God Allows U-Turns* and *God Answers Prayers,* I encourage you to visit our Web site to find out more about them. Please consider sharing your inspiring true story with us for a special collection to help empower parents and grandparents around the world. Visit www.godallowsuturns.com.

I also want to invite you to stop by our SANITY support-group Web site (visit www.allisonbottke.com and follow the links or visit www.sanitysupport.com) to locate sanity support groups in your area or to find out how to start one.

Last but not least, I'd love to hear from you. Please send an e-mail (AB@AllisonBottke. com) or drop me a letter. I respond to all correspondence if you'll give me a little time to get back to you. May God bless and keep you.

Allison Bottke
100 W. Southlake Blvd.
Southlake, TX 76092

www.AllisonBottke.com
www.GodAllowsUturns.com
www.BoomerBabesRock.com
www.SanitySupport.com

Foreword by Carol Kent

There is nothing more painful to a parent than watching your grown child experience a meltdown. Whether the process is gradual or an unexpected, sudden departure from wise choices, financial responsibility, and decent friendships, the internal reaction is the same—gut-wrenching agony as you try to figure out what went wrong when you had all of the best intentions.

You feel betrayed because as a parent, you've tried to practice unconditional love. You've offered forgiveness for inappropriate behavior and provided enough encouragement and tangible help to give your child a fresh start. But the cycle of pain continues as time after time your adult child accepts your help, promises this is the last time your assistance will be needed, and then falls flat on his or her face again—with no one to come to the rescue but you.

At such times, the enemy swoops in with taunting lies and tempts you to believe:

- *If I had been a better parent, this would not be happening.*
- *If I had read my Bible more consistently and prayed more fervently, God would have protected my child from this crisis.*
- *If I had been less busy, I could have stopped this cycle of destruction before it got to this point.*

On one level, we may feel guilty and even in some way responsible for the wrong choices of our children. Yet at a heart level we believe that even if our child's behavior doesn't warrant our support, his or her potential does! If we can just help them get out of a plummeting lifestyle and desperate circumstances, we're convinced they will finally take good advantage of their clean slate and demonstrate a new beginning that warrants all of our support and encouragement. But then, to our great disappointment, the cycle of destructive behavior begins again.

Like Allison Bottke, I'm the mother of an only child—a son. My son was not caught in a web of addiction and financially destructive behavior—but he unraveled mentally, emotionally, and spiritually when he believed his legal options for protecting his two stepdaughters from sexual abuse at the hands of their biological father had been exhausted. My husband and I received a shocking middle-of-the-night call informing us that our son, a graduate of the U.S. Naval Academy, had been arrested for murder.

After two and a half years of waiting through seven postponements of his trial, our son was eventually convicted of first-degree murder and sentenced to life in prison without the possibility of parole. I know the agony of wondering what went wrong in our parenting and of trying to "fix" things for my child so we could all go back to a more normal life.

In *Setting Boundaries with Your Adult Children,* Allison Bottke powerfully describes how subtly we begin to enable our children by "helping" them. She understands from personal experience that we parents believe our children are fundamentally good kids who have made some mistakes, so our impulse is to dive in to rescue them from the messes they've made, believing the power of love and forgiveness will conquer all of the negative choices they have made.

If you have time to read nothing else, don't miss Allison's description of walking into her son's home following his arrest in the opening chapter, "Why I Had to Write This Book." The emotional impact of her experience grabbed my emotions and made me gasp for air. If you can't read all of the chapters in a row, go to the letter she wrote (but never delivered) to her son in chapter 8. You may find pieces of your own parental emotional reactions on the pages of these chapters. But you'll uncover more than that. Perhaps for the first time you'll find a workable plan for setting appropriate boundaries with your adult child. You will discover how to form a plan of action that works. Whether your child is emotionally and/or physically disabled through addictions or wrong thinking, Allison Bottke will reveal the six steps that will bring back your SANITY. Her acrostic will help you to remember to implement new choices that will result in healing and hope for your family.

The process of setting boundaries with adult children is difficult. At times it seems harsh. The road is filled with temptations to revert back to giving financial handouts and falling back into patterns of being an enabling parent. Don't give up. Change is possible as you choose to stop the destructive cycle by placing your confidence in God, receiving emotional and spiritual support from others, acquiring additional knowledge, and consistently speaking the truth in love.

My new favorite verse is one I hope you will cling to: "See, I am doing a new thing! Now it springs up; do you not perceive it? I am making a way in the desert and streams in the wasteland" (Isaiah 43:19 NIV). My prayer is that Allison's book will launch a brand new beginning in your life. Right now, you may feel you're in a desert place as you struggle in your parenting crisis, but be alert! There's a stream in the wasteland—and you can begin making hope-filled choices that will forever change your future for the better.

Carol Kent, Speaker and Author
When I Lay My Isaac Down (NavPress)
A New Kind of Normal (Thomas Nelson)

Why I Had to Write This Book

The SWAT team left a horrible mess in their wake. Glass cracked under my feet like ice on a frozen pond, ready to break and suck me down into an abyss of frigid peace. The rancid smell of alcohol and stale cigarette smoke hung in the air like noxious perfume. The atmosphere was bathed in agony and despair. Assaulted and plundered, the house was in ruins—my heart not far behind.

It was New Year's Day. Less than 24 hours earlier, my husband and I had said good-bye to what had been a challenging year, praying the coming months would be better. Though only a few miles separated our quiet home from this catastrophic mess, I felt light-years away from comprehending how someone could live so barbaric an existence.

Yes, the SWAT team had done their share of damage in the course of duty, but it didn't take a trained eye to see that things had been far from tidy before they'd paid their surprise visit.

"It looks like the county landfill," my husband said, shaking his head.

The home had been rented to one person but appeared to have become a crash pad for many. It was obviously the site of a New Year's Eve party, and I wondered how many people had been here to celebrate only hours earlier.

What we don't notice on TV cop shows—what they can't convey after a team of highly trained police officers methodically ransack a home—is the smell of desolation that fills the air, hanging from the rafters like poisonous bats waiting to attack.

It had been weeks since I'd been inside the home, and it was not as I remembered it. I gaped at the squalor. I stood stifled against a counter in the kitchen that a few months earlier I'd cleaned and organized from top to bottom. Now the contents of the cupboards had been yanked unceremoniously from their nesting places, strewn haphazardly in heaps on the counters and floor. Like a giant petri dish, the aluminum sink held stacks of dirty dishes in a puddle of stagnant water. Shards of glass glistened in the spoiled food that clung to the plates and silverware. My stomach turned. The window behind the kitchen sink had been broken—from the outside in. It was a small window, too small for anyone to have used as a forced entry point.

"Smoke bomb," an officer said quietly as I stared and nodded.

Grease-encrusted pans sat stale on the stovetop. Beer bottles, soda-pop cans, overflowing ashtrays, and burgeoning trash cans assaulted my senses. Half-empty bottles of whisky, rum, tequila, and vodka sat upright like sentries on the counter, somehow missing the recent mêlée that still had neighbors peering from nearby windows and local thugs circling the block in their cars like sharks around a capsized boat. The front and back doors to the house had been kicked from their hinges, locks splintered and dangling like broken limbs. Kitchen drawers lay on the floor, contents tossed like debris from a fallen Dumpster. CDs, video games, DVDs, a host of electronic equipment, and stacks of clothing littered the kitchen floor. A glance toward the adjoining dining and living rooms revealed more of the same mayhem.

In the dining room, void of furniture except for a few bookcases, a large glass aquarium held two large snakes—boa constrictors, I surmised. The gentle hum of a heat lamp broke the silence. The snakes looked as out of place here as I felt. A dark foreboding began to wash over my soul, sending shivers up my spine.

"Yea, though I walk through the valley of the shadow..."

There was no escaping the facts. Clearly the SWAT team had done their work, thoroughly searching for what they had come to find, leaving little unturned.

When we arrived, an officer had indicated, "The bust was good."

"Clean," she'd called it. "He's going to have a hard time getting out of this one."

I couldn't begin to wrap my brain around that statement.

"He" was my only child—my son.

Everywhere I looked, evidence of the raid stripped my senses bare, threatening to expose the pain I choked back.

"Man, oh man, it's a total mess upstairs," my stepson said. "Wait till the landlord sees what they did. Who pays for this?" He pushed aside a pile of dirty laundry with his foot, walking through the room as though dodging land mines.

Most likely me.

My name was on the lease; they'd be coming after me.

I should never have signed. When will I learn?

"He's being booked now at the local jail, along with a few of his buddies. It's a holiday; no telling when he'll be arraigned," an officer volunteered to my husband. "You can have your lawyer call to find out."

My lawyer? I don't think so.

Shame and embarrassment washed over me, flushing my face as I watched my husband talking with the uniformed officer. A fifth-generation native of this small town with an upstanding reputation, my husband shouldn't have been pulled into this disgraceful drama. He didn't deserve this association.

None of us did.

Everywhere I looked was evidence of a life lived not on the edge but somewhere deeper—in a pathetic pit of depravity. The tumor of addiction, irresponsibility, recklessness, and crime could not be excised. It kept returning, each time more virulent than the last.

The stench of a wasted life filled my nostrils.

"Get the TV and electronic equipment out of here," I instructed my stepsons, who had come to help, as I searched the rubble on the floor for the roll of trash bags I knew had to be there somewhere. "The place will be picked clean by morning if we leave it. I doubt he'll be coming back here anytime soon. We can store his stuff at the farm until he gets out. I'll figure out what to do with the rest of it tomorrow."

"I'll see if I can secure the doors," my husband said.

Finding the trash bags, I tore one off the roll and began tossing in the putrid dishes from the sink, carefully extracting shards of glass. The alcohol came next as I emptied one bottle after another down the drain, exhibiting no amount of gentility as I threw the empty bottles into the swelling bag of refuse.

I was possessed. Raw, primitive emotion shot through my body like neon gas, lighting every fiber of my being with increasing tension. I was irrational, impervious to propriety—as though propriety mattered in the wake of a SWAT team bust!

I continued throwing away dirty cups and utensils, emptying moldy food from the refrigerator, dumping ashtrays, and collecting empty beer and pop cans. I began heaping trash bag after trash bag on the back porch.

My anger grew in proportion to the rubbish.

I marveled that a few months earlier, with the help of a dear friend, we had prepared this very space for my son's hospital homecoming. He'd survived a critical motorcycle accident and was coming home to mend multiple fractures, determined to make a fresh start. He'd returned to a clean, neat, almost pristine environment.

Looking around, I didn't believe I was seeing the same house. Then a new pain pierced my heart as my eyes turned to the lighted curio cabinet in the corner of the living room. I'd somehow missed seeing it in all my righteous indignation over the mess surrounding me.

My husband returned, with toolbox in hand, and said, "The locks are trashed, but I secured the doors until we can get someone out to fix them tomorrow. I think we should go home now, honey."

When I didn't respond, he followed my stare to the cabinet.

Deep sadness turned to anger then rage as I took in the disturbing collection of military memorabilia proudly on display—arm bands, belt buckles, helmets, flags, and photos, all carrying the black-spider insignia of the Nazi regime.

Dear God…

The weight of evil was heavy on my soul. To me, this collection represented the total opposite of all that was good, decent, holy, and just. Shrouded in illuminated silence, this abominable display shouted unspeakable expletives without uttering a word.

"Help me get this disgusting garbage out of here," I cried to no one in particular, tossing out the contents of a nearby laundry hamper so I could use it as a box.

"What do you plan to do with this stuff, Allison?" my husband asked, carrying a box on his way to my car. "Some of this looks pretty valuable; he's even got signed documents from the Third Reich. Look at this…" He stopped.

"I don't want to look!" I said. "I don't want to see it, and I'm sickened even touching it. I don't know what I'm going to do with it! Throw it away, give it to a Holocaust museum—something. I'm not leaving it here to poison someone else."

Valuable indeed; this collection represented the annihilation of countless innocent lives.

The atmosphere was heavy as we packed up the offensive collection.

"Let's get out of here now." My throat was tight as I looked around at a scene that would be forever burned on my brain.

Then, on my way out the door was another sign of how far my son had wandered. Half buried beneath the rubble of a wasted life, I picked up the plaque I'd given him long ago as a gift, and the words of Henry David Thoreau unlocked the tears of my broken heart: "If a man does not keep pace with his companions, perhaps it is because he hears a different drummer. Let him step to the music which he hears, however measured or far away."

As someone who had always felt a bit out of place myself, I'd connected with this sentiment as a young woman, growing to better understand its intrinsic meaning the older I got.

I remembered my son's words the day I gave him the plaque: "My drummer is beyond different."

Yes, my son was certainly a unique individual. On one hand, intelligent, attractive, articulate, and charismatic, and on the other, foolish, dangerous, frightening, and misguided. Yes, he was the product of a unique life. So much in fact that few of his peers were ever able to relate to him, which kept him segregated for the most part from anything that smacked of traditional influences.

With limited social and emotional skills, stunted by years of drug and alcohol abuse coupled with my maternal enabling, he had a skewed perception of reality that always afforded him an excuse for why his life was a mess.

I wondered whose fault it was this time? Who would shoulder the blame for this latest infraction, for surely it could not be a result of his choices alone.

It almost never was.

My son was nearing 35 years old, and he was seldom responsible for anything that happened to him.

It took this extreme situation and the following days and weeks for me to understand—with a clarity that broke my heart—the part I had been playing for years in the drama that was his life. And more important, what I had to do to stop the cycle once and for all.

Your story may not be as dramatic as mine. Then again, it may be worse. No matter where you fall on the continuum, if you have an adult child whose life is one crisis after another, and you find yourself entangled in his or her ongoing drama as though it were your own life, there *is* a way out.

Whether your child is 18 or 50, there are steps you can take to free yourself from the overwhelming bondage of guilt, fear, shame, anger, frustration, grief, and denial. You can (and must) get off the catastrophe carousel that has been spinning out of control for years. You can (and must) find hope and healing.

You can take back your life!

Almost a full year had passed since my son's New Year's Day arrest, and I hadn't seen or heard from him in months. I didn't know where he was living. The phone number I once had for him had been disconnected long ago, his postal box had been shut down, and his e-mail address was no longer in service.

I had periodically tried to locate him—several Web sites to search prison databases are saved on my Favorites list in my Internet browser, as if frequent searches to find out whether your only child has been incarcerated in a federal prison could be a "favorite" thing for a mother to do.

And then one night I received a phone call from a friend.

"Have you seen today's paper, Allison?" she asked.

Like a late-night phone call that sends fear coursing through your body, the tone of my friend's voice said it all. Something had happened to my son.

"No, what is it?" I swallowed, holding my breath.

"The county just unveiled a new Web site. It's supposed to help citizens identify the county's 'Most Wanted' criminals. Your son's on the list. His picture is in the paper."

I retrieved the unread newspaper and found the article, which took up the entire top half of the local news section, in color no less.

Just like the FBI, our county now has its own "Most Wanted" list.

My son's face stared out at me. His name, age, and pending charges were listed underneath. Yet his photo was the only one identified with red letters that read "Captured."

Does this mean he's incarcerated now?

I logged on to the new Web site, but strangely, the page that filled my screen no longer contained his name and photo. A continued search revealed a list of outstanding bench warrants for him and the long list of charges that had been brought against him as a result of the SWAT raid on his home. I couldn't tell if the capture the Web site referred to was recent or in reference to his year-old arrest.

Dear Lord, please continue to watch over him—Thy will be done.

I found myself looking at the other "Most Wanted" photos in the paper. Along with my son, there were 9 other males and 2 females. Except for one 54-year-old man, the remaining 11 were all in their 20s and 30s.

I couldn't help but wonder how many other parents and grandparents just like me were staring at the photo of their loved one, trying to make sense of it all, wondering how things had gone so wrong. What would we say if we were together in one room, sharing our stories of how our adult children got to this place? How many of us had been enablers of our children's disastrous choices—and how many still were?

I wondered if the other parents and grandparents had the slightest idea they weren't alone. Not by a long shot.

Some parents feel they need to shout "Unfit parent!" to those around them, so deep is their pain and guilt. But letting people in on their "secret" is unthinkable. Yet this conflict is far more prevalent than we think.

I'm just one of the many, many parents traveling this crowded, yet lonely road. I know that for most of us there are no easy answers for why things went so wrong, for how we got to this place of utter frustration and fear. We did the best we knew to do at the time. And even if we now recognize where we might have failed, there is simply no way we can alter what's happened in the past.

That may sound discouraging, but the good news is that we *can* do something to alter the future.

We *can* take back our lives—starting now.

As you begin, you should be warned that this is a book about tough love. It's about coping with dysfunctional adult children, whether male or female, living with us at home or not. It's about recognizing our own enabling patterns of behavior and learning how to finally stop the part we as parents play in the vicious cycle of repeated irresponsible behavior in our adult children.

As parents who love our children, we really do want to do the right thing—we always have—but what is the right thing? For me, the right thing turned out to be far different from anything I ever imagined.

I must also add that this isn't a book about drug-proofing your kids or a how-to manual about making rebellious kids behave. This is a book for parents who are way beyond that point. There are many helpful books available today that focus on those issues; I wish some of them had been around when my son was younger. Yet knowing what I know today, I'm not sure I would have listened to the advice they presented, so caught up in "helping" my son was I.

Not only that, but I think I had to experience every level of this epidemic of enabling in order to see clearly what was happening. God has a plan for my life and for my son's life, just as He has a plan for your life and the life of your adult child. Everything happens in its own time for a reason. I believe I had to come to the realization of the right thing to do regarding my adult child at exactly the right time.

Likewise, hopefully you are coming to the same realization of what you have to do now. That's why you're reading this book: you know something has to change, and you're ready. In the event someone has given this book to you as a gift, I pray you will keep an open mind as you read.

The truth is that I had to write this book for you—and for me. For all of us who want to break free from the stranglehold our adult children have on our hearts—for those of us who have for far too long beaten ourselves up with "What if I had…," "Why didn't I…," and "If only I hadn't…." I've learned that being hard on myself now serves no purpose and is in fact counterproductive with respect to the change that must happen.

For a long time—too long—I thought I was ready for change. I cried, whined, complained, prayed, and pretended I was ready for things to change, yet my heart of stone had not yet become a heart of flesh. I wasn't ready to do what it was going to take to change my life and, by extension, the life of my adult child.

As a result of my experience with my son and my many talks on this topic to groups of parents, I've come up with some principles I believe will work for you and for any parent willing to make the necessary changes that will result in a return to sanity. These principles, which spell out in acronym form the word SANITY, are detailed in part 2 of this book. The hope is that SANITY support groups will spring up among parents who recognize the need to regain control of their own lives, regardless of the outcome in their adult children's lives.

From my interactions with other parents in pain, I know the need for help is great. And to be honest, I think the problems we're seeing in our society with adult children not taking responsibility for their own lives are going to continue for a long time. Our society seems to be experiencing an epidemic of dysfunctional adult children. I see it everywhere.

Recently a mother and her teenage son were in front of me as I stood in line at the local Subway deli. He asked his mother if his coupon would still be valid if he split a foot-long sandwich into two six-inch subs, and she said, "I don't know; you'll have to ask."

He began to speak to the sandwich-assembly man when Mom rudely interrupted, "Can he still use his foot-long coupon if you make it a half-and-half sandwich of two different kinds?"

The young man cast his eyes downward, allowing her to speak for him.

I felt pain for him, then anger at the mom. Then a mixture of feelings washed over me, and I wondered how long she had been speaking for him and what he no doubt felt when she sent mixed messages telling him, "You can take care of this yourself," but then undermining his confidence with her "I'll handle it for you" actions. Actions that may indicate an "enabling" parent-in-training.

Earlier that same day, I was running an errand when I found myself talking to a small-business owner who was operating on her last raw nerve. We had never met, but clearly God had connected us at such a time. She was frazzled and, I suspect, another enabling parent-in-training.

In record time she was sharing her dilemma of getting no help from her two teenage sons—or from her husband. Then she mentioned in anger that she was always giving them money for this and that and never getting any change.

"They ask to borrow a 10, I give them a 20, and I never see the change!" she said.

She spoke of feeling used and disrespected, then she asked, "Couldn't they ever once pick up after themselves? Is that asking too much?"

This woman ran a successful one-woman service business; she was clearly the major breadwinner in the family. Her husband also worked a full-time job, but once he punched out for the day, he was off the clock. As a small-business owner, she worked considerably longer hours than most people.

"Why don't you think you deserve to be treated with respect?" I asked her.

She looked at me blankly for a moment, then she continued on about how her husband and kids used her, how they didn't treat her with respect, how they did this and that. In fact, she talked on and on about their issues and their needs, their troubles and their "stuff." Every time there was a break in the conversation, I turned my question back to her.

"But what about *you?*" I asked. "Why have you allowed your personal boundaries to be trampled on? Your kids and your husband don't know your boundaries because neither do you."

This made her think. Now remember, she was a total stranger; we'd never met. I was just in her shop to order something, and an hour later we were still talking, but about her life, not my reason for being there in the first place. Then again, perhaps that's exactly why I was there in the first place. God has a way of orchestrating divine appointments.

She went on to talk about her own parents—how cruel her mother had been to her when she was young, and how she vowed never to treat her children the same way.

So then I asked, "What's cruel about defining your boundaries and teaching your children right from wrong? What's cruel about setting a healthy example so your children will learn? Right now, all they know is that Mom doesn't mean what she says, that she'll always give in, that she's a walking ATM machine, and that they don't need to be held accountable for their choices or behavior...because Mom is the ever-present safety net."

I held my breath, worried I had said too much.

But after a moment's pause, she said, "You're right; I know you're right. But they're good kids. They don't do drugs or drink, they don't get into trouble—"

"And yet you're standing here telling me they're making your life miserable. That you are stressed beyond belief, that no one helps, and that you're feeling used and abused and disrespected. Is that any way to treat someone who does so much for them?"

"No, it's not," she admitted.

"So, then," I asked, "why do you keep doing for them? Why do you keep handing over the money? Why do you keep repeating the same behavior? It's *you* who has to change, not them."

She began talking more about her sons, about their issues, and then about her husband. I found myself shaking my head at the situation—because she still didn't get it.

It wasn't about her kids or her husband, or what they did or didn't do. It wasn't about changing them. It was about her ability to establish healthy boundaries and then stick to them. It's about *our* ability to do the same thing. It's about being consistent with our responses when our boundaries are violated.

We cannot change another person. We can only change ourselves and how we will respond to the good and bad behavior of our loved ones, who continue to cause us to live in daily pain.

Are you ready to set those boundaries and gain back your life?

Read on. My prayer for you is that by using the principles of SANITY, your life will change for the better.

Part One

The Parent as Enabler

There are two kinds of parents of adult dysfunctional children. The first kind are those who have apparently done everything right as parents. For these parents, the current crisis with their adult child is truly a mystery. They may even be able to point to their other adult children with pride and say something like, "We have four adult children, three of whom are living responsible, dutiful lives. And then there's our son [or daughter].... We raised all four of our children the same way. We have no idea why this child is having such a struggle."

The second kind of parent—the kind I was—is the far more common parent of an adult dysfunctional child. Somewhere along the parenting line, you (we!) set up a pattern of enabling that perhaps continues to this day. Your enabling may have been subconscious; you no doubt meant well (in fact, most enabling parents *do* mean well). But either way, the result is the same: You experience the pain of having an adult child who's out of control.

Although I spend a lot of time in this book addressing the enabling element of parenting an adult child out of control, those of you who don't see yourselves as enablers should find much help in these pages as well. For you too will have to set boundaries for your adult child. And it may happen that as you read, you'll discover subtle signals about the past that will trigger an "Aha!" or two about why your child behaves as he or she does. And, to be honest, you may be reminded of some ways in which you have perhaps adopted an enabling pattern of reacting to your child that you haven't previously recognized. It's my experience that almost all parents of dysfunctional adult children have to some extent become enablers.

So whether your parenting skills were above reproach or you realize you made some crucial mistakes with your child, this book will help you in the common task ahead: taking back your life from the pain your adult child is presently causing.

Finally, to make things easier to understand as we continue, when I use the term *adult child* hereafter, you can assume that I'm referring to the *dysfunctional* adult children whose challenging lives continually cause us grief and pain.

Let's also assume that when I refer to "he" or "him," it could just as well be "she" or "her." The enabling epidemic includes both male and female adult children. However, while no concrete data exists at present, the incidence of parents enabling *male* adult children seems to be higher, as evidenced by studies I've read, the completed questionnaires I've received, and the surveys I've conducted.

I also need to make it clear that my perspective as a parent in pain is that of a *Christian* parent in pain. I invite readers of all faiths to learn how to set the necessary boundaries you'll need to survive as a parent of an adult child in crisis, but it's my belief that a critical part of any enduring solution will be found in a firm trust in God along the way. Long ago I discovered that God knows our pain. One can scarcely read the gospel account of the pained father of the prodigal son without deep compassion for the man who walked the same path we now walk.

God knows our hearts are breaking. He knows that our adult children and their problems have become ever-present wounds that never seem to heal. And He has provided a way of hope and healing.

My prayer is that you'll find that hope and healing in the following pages.

1

"But I'm Only Trying to Help"

Let's face it, not all adult children are dysfunctional, any more than all parents are enablers. Many adult children have been raised to have deep respect for their parents and themselves. For these children, the thought of taking advantage of anyone, let alone the parents who raised them, is abhorrent. Let's call these children *functioning adult children*.

Generally speaking, functioning adult children were patterned from their youth to turn out that way, as opposed to having been patterned for dysfunctional adulthood by enabling parents. A perfect example of a functioning adult child is Dr. Dennis Hensley, author, speaker, and professor of English at Taylor University in Fort Wayne, Indiana. He recalls one memorable example of how his father helped pattern him for successful adulthood. When Dennis graduated from high school, his father gave him a clock. In an interview he told me,

> It was a four-year clock that ran backward. My dad handed it to me and said, "For the next four years, your mother and I will keep a roof over your head, food in your stomach, clothes on your back, and help you through school. But when this clock runs out of time, so do you. You're on your own after that."

I knew my dad, and I knew he wasn't bluffing. I made it
through my first four years of college living at home, but then
I left and joined the service, completing my education on the
GI Bill. It was the best thing my parents could have done.

Dr. Hensley's parents helped; they did not enable.

Another example comes from Ginger Kolbaba, editor of *Marriage Partnership* magazine and author of *Surprised by Remarriage*.
She recalls, "My parents instilled within me a strong work ethic and
a strong love for God. They helped me learn how to *think*—using
common sense, etiquette, and an understanding of the Golden Rule.
There was no sense of entitlement in my home."

Dennis and Ginger are examples of *functioning adult children,*
raised by parents who did not enable them. Oh, they most likely
weren't perfect kids growing up, but they followed a progression of
growth and independence that took them out from under the dependent care of their parents. Today, they are responsible, contributing
members of society.

Many of us parents in pain dream about seeing our adult children live as independent, functioning adults instead of the dependent,
dysfunctional adult children they have become. And no doubt many
enabling parents would argue that their adult children are incapable
of taking care of themselves. That may be true. However, is this
because of a real physical handicap or viable developmental disability,
or have years of enabling crippled your adult child? And if your child is
crippled, is this disability temporary or permanent? If temporary, what
can you do to help reverse the disability and empower your adult child
to take responsibility for himself?

The first step is for us to accept any part we may have played in
making our adult children who—and what—they've become. We
also need a better understanding of the difference between *helping*
and *enabling,* and the wisdom and willingness to make the necessary
changes *in our own lives* when at last we truly recognize the difference.

What Is the Difference Between Helping and Enabling?

Helping is doing something for someone that he is not capable of doing himself.

Enabling is doing for someone what he could and should be doing for himself.

An enabler is a person who recognizes that a negative circumstance is occurring on a regular basis and yet continues to enable the person with the problem to persist in his detrimental behaviors. Simply, *enabling creates an atmosphere in which our adult children can comfortably continue their unacceptable behavior.*

Sadly, though, the line between acceptable and unacceptable behavior is blurred for many enabling parents. Not only are we often unaware of what it means to enable, but we're equally fuzzy when it comes to what's acceptable behavior and what isn't. For instance, in the example I mentioned earlier, it *should* be unacceptable behavior for a child to ask to borrow 10 dollars and not return the change when given a 20-dollar bill. As you'll remember, the mother told me this had happened repeatedly.

When we continue to allow these behaviors, we are setting up a pattern with our children that will be hard to change. We're *enabling* their repeated inappropriate behavior. Then when we repeat the enabling pattern year after year—accepting what should be unacceptable behavior and instilling bad habits—it eventually becomes as natural to many of us as breathing. Yet all the while, a nagging feeling deep in our hearts and souls tells us something very wrong is happening. Take a moment now and look at the following sidebar. It will help you determine the extent to which you have or haven't been enabling your dysfunctional child.

By the way, a word of caution is appropriate here. In clarifying the difference between helping and enabling, I'm not saying that we can never loan our kids cash or help them out. We simply must know the difference between a responsible adult child asking Mom or Dad to loan them a few bucks when an unexpected expense pops

ARE YOU AN ENABLING PARENT?

Following are a few questions that might help you determine the difference between helping and enabling an adult child. It's interesting to note that these questions are not unlike those often asked in Al-Anon meetings when defining the behaviors of an alcoholic or drug addict with whom someone lives.

1. Have you repeatedly loaned your adult child money, which has seldom, if ever, been repaid?

2. Have you paid for education and/or job training in more than one field?

3. Have you finished a job or project that he failed to complete himself because it was easier than arguing with him?

4. Have you paid bills he was supposed to have paid himself?

5. Have you accepted part of the blame for his addictions or behavior?

6. Have you avoided talking about negative issues because you feared his response?

7. Have you bailed him out of jail or paid for his legal fees?

8. Have you given him "one more chance" and then another and another?

9. Have you ever returned home at lunchtime (or called) and found him still in bed sleeping?

10. Have you wondered how he gets money to buy cigarettes, video games, new clothes, and such but can't afford to pay his own bills?

11. Have you ever "called in sick" for your child, lying about his symptoms to his boss?

12. Have you threatened to throw him out but didn't?

13. Have you begun to feel that you've reached the end of your rope?

14. Have you begun to hate both your child and yourself for the state in which you live?

15. Have you begun to worry that the financial burden is more than you can bear?

16. Have you begun to feel that your marriage is in jeopardy because of this situation?

17. Have you noticed growing resentment in other family members because of your adult child?

18. Have you noticed that others are uncomfortable around you when this issue arises?

19. Have you noticed an increase in profanity, violence, and/or other unacceptable behavior from your adult child?

20. Have you noticed that things are missing from your home, including money, valuables, and other personal property?

If you answered yes to several of these questions, chances are that at some point in time, you have enabled your adult child to avoid his own responsibilities and to escape the consequences of his actions. Rather than helping him grow into a productive and responsible adult, you have made it easier for him to become even more dependent and irresponsible.

If you answered yes to most or all of these questions, you have not only been an enabler, but you have probably become a major contributor to the problem.

It's time to stop.

up and an adult child who *habitually* asks for money and seldom, if ever, repays it.

What I'm saying is that we need to be aware of when an adult child gets into a habit of asking for money and not repaying it, or when an adult child exhibits a sense of entitlement to his parents' money. Typically, a responsible adult child repays a loan, and the habitual borrower seldom, if ever, repays it.

The key to remember is, are we helping or enabling our adult children?

Make no mistake about it: If you have been an enabling parent, it may not be easy for you to change. Nor will any resulting changes in your adult child be easy for him to make. Learning to *choose* to do things differently isn't easy after a long-term pattern has been established.

Years ago I founded an outreach called God Allows U-Turns. A key part of that ministry is a series of true, short-story compilation books focused on ways faith can help us find new direction in life. The subtitle of that book series is The Choices We Make Change the Story of Our Life. Never is that statement more true than when deciding to change the choices we make in how we relate to our adult children who are creating pain in our lives. Equally true is that for adult children who have been consistently enabled throughout their lives, it's the choices they *don't* make that will eventually tell the story of their lives.

In her best-selling book *Raising Respectful Children in a Disrespectful World,* author Jill Rigby writes,

> Respect was paramount when we were kids. But somehow over the years we substituted self-esteem for self-respect and lost our manners. Slowly, but surely, children became the center of the universe, spoiled, egotistical and disrespectful. I often refer to them as "aristobrats."
>
> As a result of this emphasis on self-esteem, twenty-somethings are returning home rather than facing the world on their own. College kids are flunking out because they

don't know how to manage their own schedules. Kids are growing up without problem-solving skills because many of their parents think love means solving all their problems for them. Many adolescents have no respect for authority because their parents didn't command their respect. Instead, these parents gave too much and expected too little.[1]

Could this be true? Have we given too much and expected too little?

As long as we continue to keep enabling our adult children, they will continue to deny they have any problems, since most of their problems are being "solved" by those around him. Only when our adult children are forced to face the consequences of their own actions—their own *choices*—will it finally begin to sink in how deep their patterns of dependence and avoidance have become. And only then will we as parents be able to take the next step to real healing, forever ending our enabling habits and behaviors.

Assuming Responsibility for *Our* Choices

Although it's high time many of our adult children begin to accept the consequences of their choices, the plain truth is that *we must first accept the responsibility for our choices*—past choices, present choices, and future choices.

Our biggest problem isn't our adult children's inability to wake up when their alarm clocks ring, or their inability to keep a schedule, or their inability to hold down jobs or pay their bills. It's not their drug use or alcohol addictions. It's not the mess they're making of their lives. The main problem is the part we're playing in stepping in to soften the blow of the consequences that come from the choices they make.

The main problem is us.

Ouch.

It's also the excuses we make to ourselves (and others) for our enabling. Excuses like these:

- "It's just so *hard* for kids today."
- "If I don't help, who will?"
- "But I'm only trying to help."
- "No one understands my Larry [or Sally]."
- "He [or she] just needs to find the right treatment program."

Excuses like these keep us in pain—and further from any real resolution for our children or us. What must stop are the ongoing (and often useless) discussions we continue to have with our adult children, who clearly know how to push our buttons, how to control us and thus control the outcome, be it consciously or subconsciously.

The excuses must end. And as difficult as it may be to hear, we may be somewhat responsible for whatever part we've played—large or small—in the dysfunctions of our adult children. For some of us, the responsibility may be large. We have surely played a part—perhaps unwittingly—in raising disrespectful, irresponsible, ungrateful, selfish, self-centered, egotistical, and debilitatingly lazy adult children. We have played some part in raising excuse-ridden sluggards—"The sluggard craves and gets nothing, but the desires of the diligent are fully satisfied" (Proverbs 13:4).

Does this sound harsh? It was meant to. I know some of you may be saying, "Allison, please don't make me feel even more guilty about my parenting choices. I feel bad enough already."

I totally understand. However, if we really want things to change, it's time to *stop* feeling guilty, take the spotlight off our adult children, and focus ownership of the issue on ourselves. The reality of what we've done and why we've done it may be ugly, but underneath it all is something beautiful: well-meant intentions. And it's those well-meant intentions that cause us grief today.

For years some of us have focused our attention (and worries) on our adult children. We've not only taken on the role of director in the drama of their lives, but the roles of producer, stage manager, dresser, caterer, financier, and scriptwriter as well. We've done countless things for them that they are more than capable of doing for themselves. No matter whether it's a comedy, a tragedy, or a melodrama, it's time for the curtain to come down on this act.

This show is over.

But a new production is on the horizon!

We must replace our enabling behavior with something else.

Ending Enabling Behavior

From experience I've learned four life-saving truths about changing enabling behavior:

1. We can pray for the power to change ourselves.

2. We can help (not enable) adult children of any age develop wings to fly on their own.

3. We can find comfort in knowing we are not alone on this journey.

4. We can take back our lives!

In the book of James, we read, "Consider it pure joy, my brothers, whenever you face trials of many kinds, because you know that the testing of your faith develops perseverance" (1:2-3). In place of "perseverance," the New American Standard Version uses the word *endurance*. Either way we look at it, the lesson is clear: we are being instructed to hang in there, to stay the course, to *persevere* and *endure*.

What are we really made of? It's been said, "When the going gets tough, the tough get going." I've always understood the second part of that quote to mean that when we're faced with trials, we must proactively *do something*. We must *get going*, as in get up off the couch and make some positive changes. It seems others have interpreted this quote as justification to retreat, to run away from the trial, to *get going*—as in I'm outta here!

Many of our adult children have retreated from the trials and tribulations that not only test their faith but would also stretch them in ways that would develop their character, prove their mettle, and give them a sense of achievement. Consequently, many adult children have no idea what they're truly capable of accomplishing. They've never really tried to move ahead with confidence and be all they can be.

Remember, God knows when to discontinue a trial because its purpose has been fulfilled. And He gives us two great promises concerning our trials: First, His comforting presence:

> When you pass through the waters,
>   I will be with you;
> and when you pass through the rivers,
>   they will not sweep over you.
> When you walk through the fire,
>   you will not be burned;
>   the flames will not set you ablaze.
> For I am the LORD, your God,
>   the Holy One of Israel, your Savior.
>   (Isaiah 43:2-3)

And second, the assurance that He won't permit more pressure than we can handle:

> No temptation has seized you except what is common to man. And God is faithful; he will not let you be tempted beyond what you can bear. But when you are tempted, he will also provide a way out so that you can stand up under it (1 Corinthians 10:13).

The apostle Paul wrote from his experience:

> We have this treasure in jars of clay to show that this all-surpassing power is from God and not from us. We are hard pressed on every side, but not crushed; perplexed, but not in despair; persecuted, but not abandoned; struck down, but not destroyed (2 Corinthians 4:7-9).

True, he wasn't a parent of a dysfunctional child, but these verses apply to any Christian who is "hard pressed on every side" and "struck down."

And we have certainly been struck down countless times, but like the Energizer Bunny, we keep getting up. Yet we're so weary of living with the ongoing crisis that we return to the same behaviors and habits—and our adult children have us pegged. They know what to expect from us. They know that eventually we will "help" them yet again.

The bitter truth for many of us is that we haven't been helping; we've been enabling.

So instead of praying to God to stop the pain, remove the difficulty, or change the lives of our adult children, we must rise up and pray for something entirely different. We must pray for the courage to look deep in our own hearts and souls. We must pray for the strength to begin a journey that quite possibly may change our own lives—and pray for the wisdom to make new choices.

Making new choices won't always be easy. We've been repeating the same patterns for years, but now we need to ask ourselves what rewards we're getting from enabling our adult children. What need is this fulfilling in our lives?

Quite simply, we must identify our own issues.

It took me years to get to the bottom of my own issues, but once I did, things began to change.

I was 16 years old when my son was born, living a nightmare, trying to stay alive. I had run away from home at the age of 15 to marry my prince charming, except he turned out to be anything but. The first year of my son's life was like any number of Lifetime Movie of the Week scripts in which violently abusive husbands stalk their wives, making their lives a near hell on earth. One horror story after another had me looking over my shoulder for years as I tried to make sense of my world.

As a toddler, I had been brutally beaten and molested by a foster parent, which left me scarred in ways that would take me decades to sort out. I was an emotional mess before I met my first husband, then after what he did to me, I was even worse. I was only 16 years old; I had no business being a mother. I was too young, too immature, and too unstable.

But, oh, how I loved my son.

You may argue that babies have been having babies for centuries. It wasn't unusual in many cultures for girls to leave their homes as young as age 13 to begin families. However, in most of these instances, the babies were raised in households where extended family resided. Thus, a young woman learned how to become a mother from older women who were far wiser and more experienced.

Not so today. Families are spread out all over the country, and young parents are thrown into the fray with very little preparation.

Plus, the young mothers of yore seldom had the severe emotional baggage young mothers carry today. In my case, I didn't just carry baggage; I had a truckload of dysfunctions.

T. Suzanne Eller is a speaker, parenting columnist, and author of *The Mom I Want to Be.* Responding to my questionnaire, she wrote,

> Poor parenting skills are a contributing factor to the enabling epidemic. I often talk to parents whose intentions are positive, but their methods keep their adult children in a state of limbo. One parent complained that she felt her adult son would never leave home. "Why don't you tell him it's time to go?" I asked. She said that he was financially unable to support himself. This son had a nice vehicle, a Jet Ski, and trendy clothing, and he went out to eat or play often. Mom and Dad paid the mortgage, the food bills, and the utilities, and they didn't have the financial means to "play." It simply didn't make sense. This mom had no clue that they were not only teaching their adult son that others would care for him and his "needs" while he spent his money on "wants," but they were also setting him up for future relationship disasters. One day he will step into marriage, and the chances are, he will expect those he loves to continue the pattern.

It's time we break the pattern. It's time we find out what kind of parents we are and do what it takes to become the parents our adult children need.

Self-awareness of the part we play in the enabling dynamic is a major success step. When we become aware of our heart issues, we are one step closer to being healthy. And it's our own lives we must make healthy, not our adult children's lives, no matter how much we want to help them.

How they live their lives, the choices they make or don't make, and what they inevitably choose to do or not do with their future is up to them, not us. It's amazingly empowering when we begin to define and clarify our own issues as parents.

Pointing the light at ourselves is the powerful first step to changing our lives, and God willing, our adult children's lives as well.

Forgiving is good. Helping is good. Being there for our adult children is good. However, when living in constant need, crisis, or trouble becomes the rule and not the exception for our adult children, we must step back and take a look at our own lives. We must recognize our own problems with enabling and change our own patterns of behavior.

I know the idea that you may have contributed to your adult child's poor choices is uncomfortable. Perhaps some of you really haven't done much to bring about your adult child's present crisis. You may not be a chronic enabler. But keep reading. There is much for you in these pages.

Whether or not you can identify enabling behavior in your treatment of your adult child, you will still need to set boundaries in your relationship with him or her. In either case, it's no longer about your adult child; it's about you.

I know because I've been there.

And deep in your heart, you know it too.

2

Why We Enable, and Why We Must Stop

Enabling is all about boundary issues. For those of us who have our own personal issues with violated boundaries, enabling really kicks in when we become parents, as we often develop a myopic focus on helping our children, spouses, and others—anything to keep from looking at our own lives. The older our children get, the more we forget the trials and tribulations of our past and settle into a codependent way of life that is as normal to us as breathing.

We take care of people because that's just the way we are. We like to help. Never mind that it's handicapping those around us who need to learn the skills of independent living. Never mind that it's keeping us from living the lives God wants us to live.

Before I could look at the part I played in the enabling dynamic, I focused on everything except my own emotional, spiritual, psychological, or physical health. When my son was around, I smothered him with enabling behavior until he would once again run. Then I'd throw myself into another relationship, job, hobby, or project.

It has been said that we were created with two empty, needing-to-be-filled holes in our bodies. One is the stomach, and the other is the heart. My heart was damaged and empty, and I ignored the ache while I filled my stomach with food, drugs, and alcohol.

When I accepted Jesus as my Lord and Savior at the age of 35, I was on my way to a new life with a new heart, but I had a lot of the old life to sort through and throw away.

God is bigger than any issue in our past—bigger than any lie we've come to believe—but we must call on Him to help us overcome the lies that come our way on a daily basis. God knows the battles we face when we have suffered pain in our past, no matter the level.

Regardless of where you are in life, whether you feel emotionally healthy or are teetering on the edge of collapse, this is where the rubber meets the road, because for many parents in pain, if you want to move forward, you'll have to first look backward.

During my teens, when I first began to seek comfort in food and drugs, I was running from the pain of being a molested toddler and then a battered wife. I never tried to understand the pathology of abuse, nor did I seek help to deal with the pain, anger, unforgiveness, and fear that festered inside me. I learned instead to focus on other things and people; namely, on my son.

I began to live his life for him because so much of my own life was far too painful to deal with. In time I almost forgot about what it was I was trying so hard to forget about.

The New Year's Day my son was arrested, I should never have touched a thing inside his home. In my desire to come to the rescue, I once again overstepped my boundaries as a parent. After all this time, you would think I'd have known better.

It wasn't my responsibility to clean up his filthy mess or the havoc the SWAT team had left in their wake. It wasn't my responsibility to dispose of the offensive collection of Nazi memorabilia. It wasn't my responsibility to make sure that my son's personal property was safe. If vandals had come in the evening, stealing everything down to the floorboards, so be it. That would have been a consequence directly related to his actions.

I never should have dragged my husband and stepchildren into the drama, making them unwitting accomplices. I should have taken a deep breath and stepped back. I should have taken a seat in the audience, allowing the scenes to unfold in front of me instead of jumping onstage.

In "helping" my son during his crisis, I once again interfered in what very well may have been a valuable life lesson the Almighty wanted to teach him…and me.

But I know I'm not alone. Judy Hampton, author of *Ready? Set? Go!* writes,

> Paralyzed with disbelief, we did what most parents do. We tried to fix things. We tried to make our prodigal's life better. We tried rescuing and enabling. It went on for years. Why? I, for one, was an expert at it. I'd learned from an early age how to try to fix a person, even though it never really worked. But my husband and I sincerely wanted to help. And we wanted the pain to end. Admittedly, it eased some of the regret over our earlier years of poor parenting.
>
> As time passed, however, we found ourselves jeopardizing our financial future to dig our prodigal out of one hole after another. We bought cars, fixed cars, paid for insurance, cosigned for loans, lent money, paid traffic tickets, and paid for counseling. We believed the litany of excuses. The revolving door to our "rent free" house appeared to spin out of control. But nothing changed long term.
>
> "What do we do, when all we've done is just not enough?" we asked ourselves on a regular basis. The turmoil put a strain on our marriage…when we ran out of options, we hit the wall, so to speak. With no place to turn, we finally turned to God. It's rather embarrassing how long it took us to do this. Yet God, out of his mercy and grace, met us right where we were.[1]

It's a natural instinct to protect those we love, to help someone when he's down, to offer assistance during times of tribulation. Yet for some adult children, "tribulation" is their middle name. When is enough enough? Our adult children are no longer babies, toddlers, or adolescents. We must stop treating them as such. Gone are the years of trying to mold their character. Unless they decide to change as a result of changes we make (if we truly want this to stop), what we see is what we get, as the saying goes.

Even though, like me, many parents go through repeated crises with their adult children, they usually sense that something is wrong with their approach, but they never can quite put their finger on what it is.

Some parents in pain are genuinely confused about what constitutes unacceptable behavior, so ingrained is the notion that they'll do lasting psychological damage to their child's self-esteem if they establish firm boundaries with specific consequences.

Nothing could be further from the truth.

As parents, we enable because...

- we have confused "helping" with "enabling"
- we love too much, too little, too dependently, and too conditionally
- we fear for our children's safety, the consequences, and the unknown
- we feel guilty about things we did or didn't do when our children were younger
- we have never dealt with our own painful past issues, including abandonment, abuse, addictions, and a host of painful circumstances that have shaped us into who we are
- our inborn personality traits make us prone to do so
- it's all we know how to do (habit)
- sometimes it's easier to maintain the status quo than it is to change
- we think it's the right thing to do as Christians
- we make excuses because drugs and alcohol have disabled or handicapped our adult children
- we are ignorant and don't know any better

To get a better picture of what enabling looks like from different perspectives, about a year ago I distributed a questionnaire to men and women around the country. I'll refer to the results of this survey throughout the book. The respondents represent a wide demographic. Some are parents and some are not. Some have dysfunctional adult children; some do not. Their occupations include licensed counselors, professors, teachers, law-enforcement professionals, stay-at-home moms, lawyers, philanthropists, editors, authors, speakers, and clergy.

One of my questions asked the respondents what they thought was the primary reason parents rush in to "help" adult children. Listen to some of the replies and see if you could have written them:

> Fear and guilt. Fear grabs us when we think that if we say no, our adult child will make a worse mess of his or her life, and we will have to live with the pain and/or shame of those consequences. Guilt motivates us because we often feel that somehow we have failed our adult child because of something we did or didn't do when they were younger. (Leslie Vernick, author of *The Emotionally Destructive Relationship*)

> Parents who haven't dealt with their own pain and abuse—often because they don't know how to—want to "protect" their children from pain and suffering. Some parents need to first get help for their own issues before focusing on trying to help their adult children. (Georgia Shafer, licensed psychologist)

> Fear has to be among the top reasons. The range of fears likely includes at least the following: (1) fear that my child will reject me, (2) fear of what will happen to my child if I don't provide for him or her, (3) fear of what people will think, and (4) fear of living with guilt in the event that my child is harmed or harms himself or others. (Bill Oudemolen, senior pastor of Foothills Bible Church, Littleton, Colorado)

> It seems easier. It's like assigning chores when they're younger; I'd rather just do it myself so I don't need to nag them. When

they're older, it's just on a bigger scale. (Heather Gemmen Wilson, author of *Startling Beauty: My Journey From Rape to Restoration*)

Many parents are making parenting decisions based on guilt from their own inabilities and choices—choices such as working more and playing less, and their lack of availability to their children. There is also a misguided definition of what it means to "love," as in "parents who really love their children would never kick them out of their home, or refuse to bail them out of jail, or insist they pay rent, or follow rules in the home." (Jane Rubietta, author and speaker)

I know the father of a family who was raised in a children's home that was highly structured. Every child in the home was given specific work assignments, was required to attend chapel on campus, and was highly supervised through lots of rules, etc. After the father left the home and graduated from college, he married, and the couple had several children. From the get-go it was evident that the father was determined that his children were not going to be raised in the same strict and structured environment he was. The children grew up having very few responsibilities, little discipline, and too much flexibility of schedule. Today the lives of these children are chaotic, involving drugs, lack of direction, and consistently poor choices. (Arleigh M. Hegarty, pastor of counseling, Community Evangelical Free Church, Elverson, Pennsylvania)

Can you review your relationship with your adult child and identify why you have become an enabler—and to what extent? Some parents are full-blown enablers, short-circuiting their adult child's every opportunity to finally take charge of his life. Other parents may enable far less, perhaps only enough for the adult child to learn how to pull the necessary strings to set his parents' enablement into motion.

Breaking the Enabling Habit

It should come as no surprise that the first commitment a parent of an adult child must make is to stop this enabling pattern, whether large or small. It means overcoming the guilt, the fear, the regrets for past mistakes, and anything else that has caused us to become enablers of our adult children's destructive lifestyles.

Once the commitment has been made, there are two ways it can be implemented. We can simply stop enabling our adult children in one fell swoop, or we can drag it out in stages over several months or years. As one who has been there, I don't advocate the dragging-out plan.

First of all, it sends mixed messages to our adult children, and second, it's equally hard on us as parents to volley back and forth between the world of enabling behavior and the land of the clear boundaries we're trying to set. Now, that doesn't mean we act hastily without forethought. We need a plan.

In my own experience of dragging out my commitment to change, my son had come to realize that calling me from jail to ask to be bailed out was no longer an option. But he knew he could still count on Mom to send money orders so that he could have money on his "books" to buy cigarettes, toiletries, stamps, and such. In retrospect, this was a poor choice, but I justified it as "helping." I also considered it "helping" to pack, move, and store his belongings more than a few times when he was either evicted from an apartment or sentenced to serve time in jail.

Another way I mishandled my commitment to stop enabling was that after having spent tens of thousands of dollars over the years on residential-treatment programs, I committed to stop funding such programs for his supposed recovery. However, I didn't stop coming to his rescue to help him find a facility that had an open bed that he himself could afford. This often required countless phone calls he could have made himself, if indeed he was serious about getting help. I did all the legwork to the point of even helping him fill out the emergency medical-assistance forms because he had trouble understanding all of the fine print. Of the half dozen or so residential programs he's entered over the years, he has never fully completed even one program.

Then we have the cell-phone issue. Because I wanted desperately to stay in touch with him at all costs, I once signed a contract for his cell phone as long as he agreed to pay the monthly bill. He didn't have the credit history to qualify for the plan. Every month it was a battle to get him to drop off the cash or mail a money order (he didn't have a checking account). Because his phone was on my service plan, if his bill wasn't paid, my phone would also be disconnected. Don't ask me if I had to make any of those payments myself before I learned my lesson and had his phone disconnected, forcing him to find his own service plan, which he eventually did.

It's embarrassing how many times I put my foot down only to vacillate in other areas.

I cried wolf on more than one occasion, totally losing any credibility I may have had with my son.

That's what I mean when I say that dragging out your commitment doesn't work. It sends the wrong signal to your adult child.

Yes, It's Hard to Be Tough

As a psychotherapist at Oasis Counseling in Lancaster, Pennsylvania, Bill Taylor has often counseled parents to demonstrate tough love.

"Often when we speak of exercising 'tough love,'" he says, "we think of it being tough on the adult child, when in reality it's tough on the parent."

Sure, when we begin to shift gears in how we choose to respond to our adult children, life will get more difficult for them. However, the truth is that it's going to be equally painful for us as parents. We must remain "tough" in our efforts to be consistent in our new behaviors, no matter how our adult children respond.

Bill learned firsthand how hard—yet beneficial—it is for a parent to exercise tough love:

> When my oldest son was involved in some illegal activity that resulted in his incarceration, he called me several times daily, sobbing and begging me to bail him out of jail, which I could

have done and wanted to do with all my heart. I wanted to jump in my car and rush down and bring my son home. It was tough to leave him there behind bars with hardened criminals, knowing that he had to face the consequences of his actions and learn firsthand the lessons of life. But I could not enable him to get off scot-free, as much as I wanted to bail him out. It was more than tough. I sobbed each time I hung up the phone, and my heart broke for him.

Some time later after his release, he said to me, "Dad, I know it was hard for you to leave me there in jail; I want you to know I don't hold it against you. It was the best thing you could have done for me. I learned so much about myself while I was there, and I have a completely different outlook on life. And one thing's for sure…I never want to go back there again. I'm turning my life around."

Part of the commitment process for parents ready to end their enabling is the stark recognition of the pain they will experience as they follow through. As Bill Taylor cried over his son's incarceration, you will also shed tears as you move ahead with tough love. You must prepare yourself to see your child hurting.

A landmark book by Henry Cloud and John Townsend came out in 1992. It went on to sell more than one million copies and is still selling strong well over a decade later. Back then, *Boundaries* became my companion Bible study as I read and reread it, soaking up the teachings like a thirsty traveler. The doctors say,

> When we begin to set boundaries with people we love, a really hard thing happens: they hurt. They may feel a hole where you used to plug up their aloneness, their disorganization, or their financial irresponsibility. Whatever it is, they will feel a loss.
>
> If you love them, this will be difficult for you to watch. But, when you are dealing with someone who is hurting, remember that your boundaries are both necessary for you and helpful for them. If you have been enabling them to

be irresponsible, your limit setting may nudge them toward
responsibility.[2]

Tough? Definitely! But worth it in the long run.

Sheriff Richard Cook has served for three consecutive terms in his
Minnesota town. He says,

> When parents freak out that having their adult child arrested
> is the worse possible thing, I would dispel the rumor that jail
> is a terrible place to be. Our primary objective is to maintain
> the safety of the institution for the inmates and the staff. I
> also reiterate that there are programs available if the inmate
> or the accused wants to take advantage of them—if he wants
> to correct his behavior and improve his life. But the parents
> need to be aware that these are adult children who have made
> their own decisions, and those adult children must deal with
> the consequences.

Until we make the same choice to administer tough love, staying
focused on the action plan we are going to develop to stop the mad-
ness and gain SANITY (discussed in part 2), things will only continue
as usual, and they are almost certain to escalate.

Could it really get much worse?

Do you really want to know the answer to that question?

Enough Is Enough

Yes, it can get worse, *much* worse, before it gets better.

My advice is not to wait until then to make the necessary changes.
Now is the time to say enough! And I believe you do want to change
the way things are with your adult child, or you wouldn't be reading
this book.

Chances are that in the past your main goals were to help your
adult child get on his own two feet, or to help him find his purpose
in life, or to help him make better choices regarding school, work,
appointments, or finances—the list goes on. Chances are you've had

endless tearful discussions with him over the kitchen table about his options and his potential, as well as listening to one reason after another why he does or doesn't do the things he should or shouldn't do.

It's time to change your tactics. It's time to stop listening to excuses and start listening to God—and to your own instincts and intuition. Remember the difference between helping and enabling that we discussed in chapter 1? It's time to clearly define your goals as they relate to *your life,* not to the life of your adult child. You have your life and he has his life, and you must begin to live yours and he must begin to live his, without your constant interference.

Enough is enough.

We must love our adult children enough to let them go. This is what tough love is.

We must have hope that their future, as well as ours, can be filled with positive changes and abundant love.

Sheriff Cook knows what "enough" means:

> When we see parents in their last-straw mode, when they say "enough is enough," that's when things begin to change for their kids. When an adult child comes to the realization that the safety net is no longer there, he either sinks or swims. I've seen success stories for a variety of reasons, whether the adult child finds religion or a significant other who becomes a solid rock for him, or he finally hits bottom and goes to treatment and turns his life around. But this doesn't usually happen until the parents have cut him loose and are no longer there to bail him out or protect or defend him. When the parents have given up is typically when change begins.

People who learn tough love have to finally realize that their former behaviors have been enabling and that to continue in them would constitute allowing the negative pattern of their adult child's behavior to continue, and in many cases to worsen.

This is a simple truth.

There is a familiar saying many folks in AA (Alcoholics Anonymous) often repeat: "It's simple, but it ain't easy."

Deciding that enough is enough is relatively simple, but the commitment needed to experience long-lasting change is what's hard. The consistent modeling of new behaviors and the willingness to accept the consequences that will surely follow is what "ain't easy."

> When a parent places mercy above God's clear directives, they inadvertently endorse behavior that is antithetical to faith.
>
> —AUTHOR DON OTIS, IN AN INTERVIEW

In her book *Tough Love,* Pauline Neff makes frequent references to the fact that although it might not be easy, parents must begin to "work their own program," to start taking care of themselves as the first step to stopping the enabling habit. She writes,

> We must work our own program with our own improvement rather than our adult child's in mind. All we can (and should) do for our adult child is to love him, to accept him as he is, lay down the rules for living in our home, then see how it plays out.[3]

Our first responsibility as parents was to provide our babies food, shelter, clothing, and love. As babies, they were totally and utterly dependent on us.

As they grew up, our responsibilities increased to include education as we helped them learn to walk, talk, dress themselves, read, write, and so on. Imparting spiritual values to our children was crucial during this period—and a job many parents were careless about. As our children grew, we were also to instill in them by example good values, ethics, integrity, manners, and respect.

All of these parental tasks should have one result: launching our kids into the world as responsible adults who will give rather than take from society. If we did these things faithfully, chances are we've raised adult children who are productive, contributing members of society.

If, however, we have stunted their growth by neglecting one or more of these parental duties, we have fostered an environment that keeps them from living their ultimate destinies—and we are now facing a host of challenges ourselves.

In her book *It Takes a Parent: How the Culture of Pushover Parenting Is Hurting Our Kids—and What to Do About It,* author and nationally syndicated columnist Betsy Hart challenges parents to hang in there:

> Parents cannot determine good outcomes for their children. What we can determine is whether we will persevere to the best of our ability in training and guiding them toward the right end. All we can really know is that our perseverance is the best hope of seeing them reach a wholesome adulthood.[4]

No matter how old they are or how many mistakes we may have made along the parenting journey, there is still hope that with perseverance our adult children can reach "wholesome adulthood."

Our adult children didn't get this way overnight, and they won't change overnight—if ever.

But the good news is that it's never too late to begin new parenting behavior, and we can start right now. Ironically, one of the very things we can do to help our adult children is to help ourselves first. The change that comes first to us will in most cases do more for our adult children than all our ineffective enabling.

Initially, we need to identify the driving forces in our own lives. Then we need to make a commitment to modify our own behaviors. We must change not only our behaviors as they pertain to the current situations with our adult children, but we also need to change our behaviors as they pertain to our relationships with our spouses and with the other people in our lives.

If we've been in pain long enough, chances are we're weary, angry, guilt-ridden, fearful, resentful, bitter, filled with self-pity, ashamed, indignant, disgusted, terrified, hurting, embarrassed, defeated, depressed, and weak.

It's time to put an end to all those adjectives and establish patterns that will bring a host of new ones into our lives. Adjectives like *peaceful, confident, happy, hopeful,* and *free.*

Learning to Truly Trust God

Once we make a commitment to true change, the single most important step we must take is to hand the problem—all of it—over to God. Perhaps in the past we've prayed something like, *Okay, God, he's all Yours. There's nothing more I can do. I'm going to wash my hands of the entire mess and trust that You'll take care of things in Your own time.*

Believe me, I can understand this prayer of total defeat, and washing our hands of the entire mess may be just what we want to do at this point. But as far as "there's nothing more I can do," I disagree. There is a great deal we *can* do—and a great deal we *must* do when we reach this critical point of surrender. We can focus on God's ability to do what *we* never could do.

On the questionnaire I sent out, I received this response from author Kathi Macias on the importance of faith in the process of ending the enabling pattern:

> One of the Scriptures that helped me more than once during the challenges with my son was John 21:15, where Jesus asks Simon Peter, "Do you truly love me more than these?" How many times did I hear those words echo in my heart when I was tempted to cross my own boundaries and enable my son! When I neglect my relationship with the Lord in any way and that relationship cools and slips from first place in my life, I slip—I cross back over into my old enabling patterns and start trying to fix, rescue, control, and manage…and it never, ever works.

Kathi understood that her relationship with the Lord kept her anchored in her commitment to no longer enable her adult child and that when she faltered from focusing on her faith, she was prone to crossing back over to her old patterns of behavior in response to her son.

The second question on my Parents in Pain questionnaire asked, "What advice would you give to a parent who is about to implement new boundaries to stop enabling their adult children?" I received a great response from Arleigh Hegarty, pastor of counseling at the Community Evangelical Free Church in Elverson, Pennsylvania:

> I would work with the parent regarding God's sovereignty over, and His ability to provide for, their adult children after they draw the line and begin to implement new boundaries, which may include asking their adult child to leave their home. Parents tend to become immobilized by the what-ifs, and fear hinders their making the hard decision of putting their children out on their own.

As we break off our pattern of enabling our children, it's imperative that we fully understand what it means to have a sovereign God. We need to understand the countless ways God has assured us that He will provide not only for our children but also for us, and our marriages, and our friendships, and all things.

Handing our adult children over to God means more than simply giving our adult children to Him. It means giving ourselves to Him. It means developing a relationship with Him through His Word and through prayer. Far from being a passive activity, handing over our children and their situations to God requires a very active commitment on our part. We are to exercise faith that our sovereign God will do what must be done in our lives and in the lives of our adult children.

Here's what Henry Cloud and John Townsend say about our relationship with God:

> Relationship is what the gospel is about. It is a gospel of "reconciliation" (Rom. 5:11; Col. 1:19-20). This gospel brings hostile parties together (Col. 1:21) and heals relationships between God and humanity, and between people.

The gospel brings things back to their created order, the truth and order of God. In terms of relationships, we think that God's order of relationship is himself and the way he works. And that is why we think boundaries are so important, because he has them and we are to be redeemed into his image.

Boundaries are inherent in any relationship God has created, for they define the two parties who are loving each other. In this sense, boundaries between God and us are very important. They are not to do away with the fundamental oneness or unity that we have with him (John 17:20-23), but they are to define the two parties in unity. There is no unity without distinct identities, and boundaries define the distinct identities involved.

We need to know these boundaries between us and him. Boundaries help us to be the best we can be—in God's image. They let us see God as he really is. They enable us to negotiate life, fulfilling our responsibilities and requirements. If we are trying to do his work for him, we will fail. If we are wishing for him to do our work for us, he will refuse. But if we do our work, and God does his, we will find strength in a real relationship with our Creator.[5]

Ah, to find strength! I can't begin to tell you how many times I prayed for strength to get through another crisis with my son. However, it wasn't until I stopped praying for strength and began to recite the familiar Serenity Prayer, made memorable by Alcoholics Anonymous, that I began to experience real healing and hope: *"God grant me the serenity to accept the things I cannot change, the courage to change the things I can, and the wisdom to know the difference."*

In AA, for the friends and family of an alcoholic, the key to serenity is finding the wisdom to know the difference between what they can and cannot change. The same holds true for parents in pain who have enabled their adult children time and again, whether or not the adult children have issues involving drugs or alcohol.

We must stop trying to change their behaviors by making choices for them and by shielding them from the painful consequences of their actions or inaction. We cannot change them.

However, we can change ourselves—and that is where we must begin.

"But I can't abandon my child," you say.

Setting our adult children free to live the lives God intended them to live is *not* abandonment—even if it means setting them free during a time of severe trial and tribulation in their lives.

Consider the story of the prodigal son in the Bible. A rich young man left his family, squandered his inheritance in a foreign land, and ended up wallowing in a pigsty. Destitute and near death, he got up and went home, where his loving father met him with open arms, and they lived happily ever after. Yet please note that nowhere in the story does it say that the loving father ever ran after his son.

Prodigals, by the way, come in both genders. In her thought-provoking book *If the Prodigal Were a Daughter,* the late Janice Chaffee gave readers a broader view of the prodigal story:

> This ancient story is good and exemplary for boys. But what about girls? What is the modern story of a Prodigal Daughter?
>
> I picture her as an honor-roll high-school graduate turned wild party-girl expelled from college. Abandoned by her first love after an abortion, she sedated herself in a downward spiral of alcohol, drugs, and promiscuity. She bounced from one job to another, had an affair with a married man, and then left the country to escape disappointment and loss. Years later, lonely, weak from an eating disorder, and painfully aware of her emotional, physical, and spiritual bankruptcy, she returned to her father's home to ask for forgiveness.[6]

Although the father in Jesus' parable didn't chase after the rebellious son, we do see that he *watched* for his son's return. He was hopeful. Expectant. Handing our children over to God is the safest and most meaningful thing we can do to end the cycle of enabling. We must stop continually running after our adult children and start taking care of ourselves. God willing, they will return home one day, ready, willing, and able to live lives of honor.

Do not underestimate the power of God to restore your adult child.

Although there is certainly no improving on the original Ten Commandments in Exodus 20, I've developed another helpful top-ten list of commandments (or suggestions) when it comes to breaking the enabling cycle.

The Lord gave us the Ten Commandments as foundational principles by which to live our lives. Combine them with the ten suggestions below, and you will be well on your way to gaining SANITY in the insane world of enabling.

Allison's Top-Ten Suggestions for Breaking the Enabling Cycle

1. You shall take care of your own spiritual, mental, physical, emotional, and financial health.

2. You shall remember to express love and attention to your spouse and other family members and friends in addition to your troubled adult child.

3. You shall not accept excuses.

4. You shall understand that a clear definition of right and wrong is imperative for a disciplined society. There is no room for gray. Don't make excuses for what you believe.

5. You shall make fact-based judgments without excuse and feel okay doing so.

6. You shall uphold standards of behavior that protect your morals, values, and integrity.

7. You shall give your adult child unconditional love and support without meddling and without money.

8. You shall listen to music and read books that will focus your mind on God.

9. You shall celebrate life and love as often as possible, even in times of trouble.

10. You shall consistently practice the six steps to SANITY as outlined in part 2 of this book.

3

Get Smart and Take Action!

Enabling parents know that we live either smack dab in the middle of crisis or we're simply in between crises, waiting for the other shoe to drop. Every time the phone rings at night, we are catapulted to a place of despair. Will it be our adult child in a drunken stupor, will it be the police, or will it be the morgue?

Let's look at these two ways we live and what we need to do to implement the decision we've made to stop enabling and set boundaries for our adult children.

1. *In between crises.* Without a doubt, this is the best time to put our decision into motion. We would be wise to develop our action plan during this time, then present it to our adult children and get out of the way.

2. *In crisis mode.* This is a harder time to implement your decision, but it can also show an immediate effect. If, for instance, your adult child has been arrested, do not intervene this time. If your adult child lives at home and is involved in anything related to drugs, alcohol, crime, violence, unacceptable behavior, or any type of illegal activity whatsoever, insist on his immediate departure from your home. Call the authorities if necessary. He can choose to go to rehab or to a friend's home, or anywhere he'd like, including living on the street—whatever he decides—but it is *not* your responsibility to find

somewhere for him to go. Remember, if he has broken the law, you may be considered an accessory to his crime. Calling the police will be one of the hardest things you'll ever have to do, but it may be necessary.

If your adult child lives outside the home and is calling for money or a place to live, or is requesting (in many cases, begging) for your signature on a contract or rental agreement, do not give it to him.

There's an old saying, "You can't paddle another man's canoe for him." We've been paddling our adult children's canoes for far too long. It's time they learned how to paddle for themselves.

Knowing that we need to change and taking the steps necessary to make changes are, sadly, often two entirely different things. Let's look at a very real family dealing with a very real situation. This couple sought my advice when I shared my situation with them and told them about the book I was working on that would help parents establish proper boundaries with their adult children. Names have been changed to protect their privacy; any resemblance to your situation is purely accidental. Their story is typical of many.

Stan and Sandy

Stan and Sandy have been happily married for almost 30 years. Like many couples, they married in their early 20s, fresh out of college. They've had their ups and downs over the years, but they've weathered every storm. Standing firmly together in their faith in God and in their commitment to their marriage has been a source of strength for them and for their three children—all of whom still live at home.

Both Stan and Sandy are hard-working, church-going, educated adults. They live comfortably in middle-class America—not extravagantly by any means—and they truly want what is best for their children.

Ivy is their late-in-life child, and at 10 she is a precocious yet studious girl. She loves school and talks of being a doctor. She doesn't cause her parents one iota of trouble.

In his last year of high school, Cliff, their 17-year-old son, has a tender and loving heart, with aspirations of being a minister. He says he's keeping his options open for what he wants to do with his life, but lately he's been sending away for school literature and financial-aid forms from Bible colleges around the country.

Their firstborn, however, is another story entirely.

At 25 years old, Roger is still trying to find himself.

But finding himself seldom happens on most days until well after noon because he likes to sleep in. After all, he stays up most nights playing video games, watching movies, or surfing the Internet, and he needs a full eight to ten hours of sleep to fully function, or so he says. This week he's working part time at a local pizza parlor, but he changes employment like he changes his socks, which his mother still washes on her day off.

Roger's room, comfortable to the extreme, is in the lower walk-out level of their home, adjacent to the family room. His parents remodeled the home seven years ago when Roger graduated from high school, giving him a somewhat private environment in which to live. He'd like to get his own place one day, but how can he afford it making minimum wage working part time?

An intelligent young man, Roger doesn't do drugs or drink, from what his parents can tell, and he's always home at night. They believe strongly in his potential, knowing for certain that once he finds his niche in life, he will go far.

And so, in search of that nebulous niche, they have funded numerous college courses, technical schools, and art classes when he recently decided he wanted to be an artist. But he quit going to those art classes when they interfered with a weekly reality-TV show he wanted to watch.

With every new endeavor they fund for their son, these loving, well-meaning parents establish guidelines indicating that he will maintain a certain grade-point average, lest no more tuition funds be made available. But Roger has eventually dropped out of every school, program, and course he's started, citing more than one excuse, quick to convincingly explain his more than justifiable reasons for doing so. Picture a large metal wheel in the cage of life, and Stan and Sandy are the human gerbils running in circles. The guidelines they developed could just as well be shredded and used to line the bottom of their gerbil cage. They never mean what they say, and their son knows it. They epitomize parents who continually cry wolf.

"I know we have a problem," Sandy admits, "but we don't know what to do. The last time Roger quit school, we told him we were finished paying for any more education. If he wanted to take classes anywhere, he'd have to pay for them himself. But Stan gave in, and now we're paying tuition at another college."

> *The Definition of Insanity:*
> Repeating the same thing and expecting different results.

Roger is more than willing to sit down and discuss his options and choices with his parents—something they've done with him ad nauseam for years. Endless discussions filled with excuses, justification, and rules with no consequences. But more damaging than these useless discussions is that when Sandy is strong, Stan is weak, and when Stan is firm, Sandy's maternal heart melts for her son's situation.

As we hear their story, it soon becomes obvious that something has to change. And unless Stan and Sandy can get on the same page and stay there—presenting a united front and establishing firm boundaries—their son will be 30 years old and still living at home, "looking to find himself" while his parents continue to support him financially and emotionally.

"What about *our* life?" Sandy asked. "We've worked hard, Stan is looking at a possible early retirement, and don't we deserve to reap some of the rewards of our years of hard work?"

As they shared their story with me, their pain was clear. Sandy looked to me for validation that what she was feeling was okay, that she wasn't being a horribly selfish parent for thinking this way.

I was honest with her as I said, "I can't tell you what to do, Sandy, but I can tell you this. The spotlight must be taken off Roger and focused instead on you and your husband. You two need to get strong, individually and as a couple, and let this 'boy' take responsibility for his own life. You need to get outside help to find out why both of you continually make choices that are crippling your son—why you are willingly handicapping him."

Judging by the hurt look on Sandy's face, I knew my words had surprised her. I admit it, I'm not very coy when it comes to this issue. I suppose I could have been more gentle in my admonishment, but I've heard this same story repeated so many times. What's it going to take for us parents to get a clue?

It's going to take determination, hard work, and commitment on our part to stop playing our adult children's games. And, of course, it's also going to take a great deal of effort on the part of our adult children to change. But it's up to them to make the choice to change. Either they will do what it takes or they won't. Once again I repeat, the goal is not to try to fix them but instead to fix ourselves.

That is why

- we must not retreat;
- we must be committed to changing our responses;
- we must have an action plan; and
- we must follow the Six Steps to SANITY detailed in part 2 of this book.

Taking Action

As might be expected, the actions Stan and Sandy need to make will not be popular with Roger. He will almost certainly accuse them of not loving him or of being selfish themselves, or he will make any other number of untrue assertions designed to get them to resume the game they've all been playing for so long.

One young woman, whom I'll call Sarah, related her anger when her parents established boundaries in her life:

> I was pretty ticked off at my parents when they closed my

checking account and canceled my credit card. But look-ing back now, it was the best thing they could have done. I was blowing it, and I think on some level I knew it, but it was kind of like smoking, you know? We know it's bad for us, but it's a hard habit to break. I had to drop out of a few classes and take another part-time job, but all that talk about gaining self-respect and becoming empowered turned out to be true. The more I accomplished on my own, the better I felt.

Change Can Be Freeing—or Frightening

When we make the decision to release our adult children to fend for themselves, it can be both freeing and frightening. For many of us, this sudden freedom to live our own lives will seem like a breath of fresh air. For others, it will bring deep foreboding and fear.

What will we do when we stop living our adult children's lives for them?

We will start living our own.

On my journey to freedom from enabling, I've found the follow-ing ten steps helpful:

1. Memorize the Ten Suggestions for Breaking the Enabling Cycle (see page 59). You'll need to remind yourself of these often. Having them just a thought away will be very helpful in time of need.

2. Make becoming healthy a personal goal. Decide from this moment on to become stronger spiritually, emotionally, psy-chologically, financially, and physically. If you're married, make the commitment to strengthen your union. Get coun-seling or join an appropriate support group, if necessary.

3. Decide to live *your* life and to stop living the life of your adult child. Find a hobby, join a gym, volunteer, or take a dance class. Do something you've always wanted to do.

4. Take a step back and view the situation with your adult child from an unemotional perspective. Write a bio about

your adult child as though you were not his parent but instead were a bystander who has been watching from afar for months. What is your adult child really like?

5. Develop your action plan. This written document will clearly state the things you plan to change and will include nonnegotiable rules and boundaries, firm but reasonable consequences, and time frames. If you're married, you should do this as a couple. Remember, you and your spouse must agree on all areas of your plan and be prepared to present a united front at all times. If you're a single parent, get help from a support group or from an accountability partner. Detailed guidelines to help you develop an action plan can be found in chapter 12 "Developing an Action Plan."

6. Prepare yourself for worst-case scenarios. Taking a stand often precipitates a crisis, and the situation may get worse before it gets better. Think of this like an emergency fire drill and carefully plan your course of action in as many scenarios as possible. Role play with your spouse or a close friend. Stand firm!

7. Commit to being consistent—*Do not back down, do not negotiate.* It could take days, weeks, months, or years for your adult child to change, if ever. There's no way to tell. He may never change—*but you have.* Prepare to wait it out.

8. Stay connected to your support group and ask for help when needed.

9. Read the Bible along with a Bible study. Do this with a group, if possible.

10. Pray, and always remember to "let go and let God."

I can hear many of you saying, "That sounds great in theory, Allison, but I don't have time in my life right now to follow a list. Things are falling apart around me, and life is out of control."

Most parents in pain know this feeling. If your present crisis has so incapacitated you that you must make important choices prior to starting your plan—if it is indeed that bad—I strongly suggest you seek the advice of a professional interventionist or a member of a support group right now. You don't want to repeat a response or behavior that hasn't worked before. It's time to do something different.

Here are a few circumstances that typically send us into crisis mode:

- We discover drugs in our home.
- Our adult child has been arrested.
- Our adult child has been hospitalized.
- An urgent issue concerning our adult child has sent our family once again into hyperalert status.

A few months before the SWAT raid on my son's home, he was in a critical motorcycle accident. It happened on a deserted country road very early in the morning. He was alone, he'd been drinking, and he wasn't wearing a helmet. When his cycle went off the road, it rolled over on him, crushing his right hand, dislocating his shoulder, breaking his leg, and leaving him bruised and battered. He managed to make a call on his cell phone before losing consciousness. Just a few days before, he had moved into a rented single home a few miles from us. His belongings were still in boxes.

My husband, Kevin, and I arrived at the hospital ICU to find him hooked up to multiple machines and being carefully monitored for possible head or spine trauma, of which there ultimately was none.

Surely, God has a plan for you, I once again thought.

Over the course of the next few days, I went into hover mode, forgetting everything I had learned about how not to enable. I rented a room across from the hospital so I didn't have to drive the 75 miles every day, allowing me to remain in his room most of the day. Without medical insurance, he needed to apply for emergency care, and because he couldn't hold a pencil to write, I helped him complete the forms. Now this wouldn't be considered enabling, because he could not in fact hold a writing implement himself. However, I became not only his hands but his mouth as well, and at times his mind, too, as

I began making choices for him that he clearly could have made for himself.

With the help of a friend of mine, while my son recuperated in the hospital, we unpacked his belongings and cleaned his home in preparation for his return. I did the legwork to rent a hospital bed, tray table, portable toilet, and walker. My husband and sons built a ramp on his back stairs for wheelchair access to his house. I arranged for a visiting home health-care nurse to look in on him and scheduled physical therapy for him. I shopped for groceries the day he came home from the hospital. I instructed his girlfriend-of-the-moment how to take care of him. I was worried sick that he wouldn't take care of himself. Yet why should he when he had me taking care of him?

Long story short, by the time my son came home from the hospital, he had fallen off the drug-use wagon, becoming once again addicted, this time to Vicodin, oxycodone, and morphine. His friends of questionable character, who never seemed to work, started hanging around, and instead of eating and sleeping right, taking care of himself, and doing what he needed to do to get better, he fell into depression, excessive drug use, and God only knows what else.

He wouldn't answer his phone, the curtains were always pulled, the home was dark and smoke-filled, and the floor was littered with trash and beer bottles whenever I stopped by.

I stopped stopping by.

After weeks of beseeching him to get help, to take care of himself, and to stop his downward spiral, I once again had to step out of the picture, handing him over to the Lord for safekeeping—something I should have done the day I walked into the ICU at the hospital.

Oh, I prayed—a lot. I called my pastor, and he visited my son in the hospital and prayed over him. My dear friends were praying for him en masse. Perhaps they should have been praying for me. I had once again fallen into the pattern of being my son's enabler. I should not have become so overly involved in trying to take care of him. He had been driving a motorcycle under the influence of alcohol—without wearing a helmet. He was blessed to be alive, blessed that he didn't kill himself or someone else. In truth, the thing he needed most, after medical care, was to accept the consequences of those actions on his own.

It's not easy to stay strong when a crisis occurs. I wasn't prepared. Today I would do it differently. If it ever happens again, God forbid, I'll behave differently. I only wish now, in that retrospective wisdom we all know and love, that I had known the value of role-playing different crisis scenarios before this happened.

We'll talk later about role playing and how important it is to go over every conceivable consequence to your actions as you develop your action plan and begin to change your behavior to stop your enabling.

But for right now, in order to get smart and take action, you must be ready to declare the following:

> As of today, I will no longer be...

- an enabler to someone who has no self-respect or respect for me
- a rescuer to someone who has no desire to be rescued
- a caregiver to someone who is capable of caring for himself or herself

I can hear you asking, "But what will happen if I stop doing all these things I've done all these years to 'help'?"

I don't know, but let me ask you a question: Has what you've been doing all this time been helping—really?

Al-Anon members learn that no individual is responsible for another person's disease or recovery from it. The simple answer as to what to do about the alcoholic holds true for what to do about the adult child we've been enabling: "let go and let God."

So we must *get smart and take action*.

4

"But Deep Down He's Really a Good Kid"

"Johnny's basically a good kid just trying to get it together."

If only I had a dollar for every parent who has said that to me!

The only trouble is that for Johnny, "getting it together" doesn't happen until he wakes up, usually well into the day, at which time he eats (leaving the dirty dishes in the sink). Then he spends time playing video games or surfing on the Internet or wondering why his mother didn't get around to washing his clothes yet.

It's hard for some parents in pain to recognize and admit that who and what our children *used* to be is not who and what they are *now*. Metamorphosis has occurred, and we've not wanted to see it. Many of our adult children are emotionally, intellectually, psychologically, socially, and spiritually stunted. Many are so rebellious, our hearts repeatedly break, and still other children are dangerously fragile, hanging on by a thread. Some have become unrecognizable to us. Some have gone from smoking pot to selling it. From destroying their own lives to taking others with them, like siblings, peers, and even innocent bystanders, who are affected by the destructive behavior of our adult children, such as causing vehicular accidents while driving under the influence.

Many of these adult children have cost their parents their marriages, their jobs, their financial health, their sanity...and in some cases, even their faith in God.

When it comes right down to it, we must come to grips with reality: our adult children's very costly "rebellious streaks" aren't just phases that will go away. However, that doesn't mean our children are lost causes. Far from it.

In *After the Locusts,* Jan Coleman skillfully weaves lessons from the Old Testament book of Joel with powerful stories of ordinary people who found renewed meaning for their lives after the locusts paid an unwanted visit. Many, like beloved author and speaker Liz Curtis Higgs, look at their ruined dreams and wasted years as the first heartbeat of what would become vital ministries helping others up and out of their struggles.

As long as our adult children are alive, there is still hope for them—hope for their redemption, salvation, and return. Restoring ruined dreams and reclaiming wasted years is what God does best. It's the topic of Jan's book and the prophet Joel's entire message: "I will restore to you the years that the swarming locust has eaten" (Joel 2:25 NKJV).

We do not parent as those who have no hope. We have a God who watches over our children—if we'll just get out of His way and let Him do the restoring. Restoration is such a promising word to parents in pain. But to get to restoration, we must start with the truth of where we are. We must be honest. The truth is that those once-innocent children grew into the jaded and unmotivated adults they are today under our parental watch. And now we find that one huge step in the restoration process is to honestly see our adult children for who they really are *now,* not as we remember them in their Kodak moments.

Many of our adult children are lost in bondage. Habitual drug and alcohol usage at a young age often stunts the social and emotional skills of users. An adult child may be 25 years old chronologically, but socially and emotionally he's still in junior high, perhaps even grade school.

Stunted social and emotional skills could also appear in instances where drug and/or alcohol abuse did not take place, where instead of chemical dependency, an adult child has grown overly dependent on parents or other guardians. In some cases, *we* have become the drug that numbs our children's pain.

For many enabling parents in pain, the decline of character in our adult children did not occur overnight. The progression has been happening for many years, in many instances right under our noses. The view many of us have of our adult children is often of the precious son or daughter we raised—an innocent babe filled with potential, eager to please.

We must wake up.

This distorted view isn't helping our children to become the adults God wants them to be. To get past this, we must become objective while retaining an ability to love. Being able to see our situation clearly is critical as we move forward.

In her book *Prodigal in the Parsonage,* Judi Braddy candidly shares the painful journey she and her minister-husband experienced as parents of children whose choices included running away, drugs, alcohol, violence, anger, and premarital sex:

> Heaven knows what has happened in our children's lives. However, rest assured: God is not just present—he's active in all our lives. More is happening in the heavenly realm than we can possibly know.
>
> This means coming to see our situation not as punishment but as a journey God will make with us. That requires us, then, to make a choice as to whether we'll allow our emotions to overwhelm us, making us bitter and disillusioned, or filter them through prayer and the Word.
>
> By doing the latter, we free ourselves to move ahead, committed not just to fulfilling our duty to ministry—this is way bigger than that—but also to our devotion to living out God's heavenly purpose on earth. In addition, like any good father, he promises a gift to keep us going. His peace passes earthly understanding.

Only then will our question no longer be "What in heaven's
name has happened?" but "How will God use us for heaven's
sake?"[1]

As Judi says, we must look at our situation not as punishment but
as a journey God will make with us.

The time has passed to ask, "What in heaven's name has happened?" The question must now be "How can I change in order to
love God, myself, and my adult child in healthy ways?"

I married my husband, Kevin, when I was 39 and my son was
23.

I asked Christopher to walk me down the aisle, my first church
wedding—a marriage I felt certain was sanctioned by God.

My son looked so handsome in his tuxedo, but so thin. Hard-core
drug addiction will do that to you, although at the time I was clueless.
I was still seeing him as I wanted to see him.

He'd disappeared just before the service began, leaving me standing in the church narthex waiting.

"Hey, Momza! Ready for the big walk?" he asked when he
returned.

His smile was broad, infectious; his eyes glazed and rheumy.

It was a beautiful service, made all the more special by the presence of my mother in the front row, my sister, who was my matron
of honor, and my close friend Linda, who had flown in from Arizona
to join the celebration.

At one point during a prayer, I glanced over my shoulder to see
my son standing with his hands clasped in front of him, his back to
the audience, eyes heavy. He appeared to be swaying. Was he high
on something? At my wedding?

Until then I'd thought the extent of his drug use was marijuana.
I had no idea he was battling a war with heroin, one of the deadliest
drugs of the time.

My son is a brilliant young man with an excellent command of
the English language. He's bright, articulate, and funny—when he

isn't drunk, high, or angry. He was a sweet and precocious young boy; many people will tell you how much they enjoyed being around him when he was young—*but that's not who he is anymore.*

I've seen his cornflower blue eyes go from laughter to a cold, terrifying glare, a look I imagine he mastered in jail, prison, or on the streets when his very life depended on his ability to instill fear in the heart of an opponent.

"You don't want to know what I've seen," he once told me.

I imagine I don't.

Yet is all my enabling going to help erase the bitter and painful memories he carries in his mind and heart? No. Only God can do that, and I am not God. I must get out of the way and let God do what only He can. I must temper compassion for my son with wisdom. And I must not confuse compassion with sentimentality.

We parents want to see our adult children as good and decent even though they're not. We as parents have to be disciplined and smart enough to admit when our preconceived notions are wrong.

In her response to my questionnaire, author Brenda Nixon wrote,

> We must try to "pull away" and observe our children as separate adults. Then we need to ask ourselves, "Would I allow, excuse, or enable this adult's behavior in any other situation?" This emotional distance may provide objective insight and the needed energy to change our behavior so we stop enabling our children.

The following might be a painful exercise.* Carefully answer each question truthfully. You are doing no one, least of all your adult child, any favors by sugar-coating the painful reality. If you are unable to be objective, ask someone close to the situation to help. However, don't get angry with the person if he or she tells you things you don't want to hear.

---

* Although I refer to "he" throughout these questions, they are certainly applicable to female adult children as well.

1. Truthfulness: Does my adult child tell me the truth about his activities? (Or have you caught him in lies on more than one occasion?)

2. Temperament: Does my child have an even temper? Or is he prone to mood swings? Does he often display irritability, annoyance, and impatience? Does he withdraw from interactions with others?

3. Empathetic: Is my adult child able to empathize with the hurts of others or is he most likely unaware of others' pain or unable to identify with their plight?

4. Personality: Which word best describes my child: warm or cold? Is he often personally cold toward other people....or is warm and inviting to people he meets?

5. Selflessness: Which word is more accurate in describing my child, "humble" or "prideful"? Is he egocentric? Cocky? Does the world revolve around him and his own desires, or is he able to give himself to others to help meet their needs?

6. Emotionally stable: Is he able to handle his emotions maturely....or do his emotions (anger, depression, guilt) drive his actions?

7. A healthy conscience: Is my child able to feel the appropriate guilt for his wrong actions? Or is guilt something he rarely feels or tries to rationalize away by placing blame elsewhere?

8. Independent: Is he more independent or dependent? Does he consistently see that his needs are met through his own efforts or must he rely on others to supply his needs?

9. Physically responsible: Does he treat his body with respect....or is he careless about his health?

10. Responsibility: Is my child assuming full responsibility for his life? (Does he follow through on promises made? Are bills paid on time? Does he show up on time for work?)

11. Accepting blame: Does my child blame other people, adverse circumstances, or even God for his woes….or does he fully accept his part in creating the life he now lives?

12. Genuineness: Is my child transparent about who he is…. or does he wear masks? Does he turn on the charm when necessary to get his way?

13. Optimistic: Is my child generally optimistic? If so, is his optimism grounded in reality or based on unreasonable suppositions? Or is he generally pessimistic about the future?

14. Trusting: Does my child find it easy to trust others, or is he generally suspicious of others?

15. Sexually responsible: Is he sexually responsible or does he engage in many short-term sexual relationships with different partners? Has he fathered a child for whom he must be responsible? Has his promiscuity resulted in abortions?

16. Ambition: Does my child show any evidence of wanting to be a successful adult? Does he set goals and work toward them…or is he wandering through life aimlessly, with no desire to succeed in life?

17. Self-control: Is my child able to control his actions when he wants to? Or does he fall easily when tempted? Is his behavior often reckless?

18. Builds successful relationships: Is my child able to build and maintain healthy relationships with other people? Or are most of his relationships short-term? Does he have a hard time making commitments in relationships?

19. Never abusive: Does my adult child resort to physical, verbal, sexual, or emotional abuse when it serves his purposes?

20. Law-abiding: Does my adult child respect the law? Or does he bend or even break the law when it serves his purposes? Does he take pride in his ability to do so?

A sociopath has something wrong with his conscience. Either he doesn't have one, or it's severely fragmented or corrupt. Today, politically correct psychologists often call this a *character disorder,* typically defined as a condition in which a person doesn't want to take responsibility for his own actions and life. As with any psychological disorder, there are varying degrees to which a person is affected. It's almost incomprehensible and beyond painful to think of our adult children in these terms. Yet some of us must.

Some of our kids are no longer hanging around with a bad crowd; they *are* the bad crowd.

Sociopaths only care about fulfilling their own needs and desires— selfishness and egocentricity to the extreme. Everything and everybody are mentally twisted around in their minds as objects to be used to get what they want. Your adult child may or may not have some level of antisocial personality disorder.

Antisocial personality disorder (abbreviated APD or ASPD) is characterized by the disordered individual's disregard for social rules and norms, impulsive behavior, and indifference to the rights and feelings of others.

Not surprisingly, parental failure (most often fatherlessness) is cited as a key factor as to why someone develops a sociopathic personality. Of course, there are many reasons why our adult children have become corrupt in their thinking, behaviors, attitudes, and choices.

And surely any knowledgeable parent—particularly a Christian parent—will have to acknowledge the reality and powerful influence of evil. As Christians we understand Satan's ability to corrupt and destroy a human life.

Our children, however, are not beyond our prayers. On the contrary, now is the time we must pray all the harder. By setting in motion a plan whereby we cut the cord of enablement, we are releasing our adult children into a world where they can sink or swim, but we are also releasing them into a world where we can all, parents and children alike, fully realize the power of God to work in miraculous ways to bring His children out of bondage and into lives of freedom and peace.

Removing the Blinders

A mnemonic device that can be used to help us remember the criteria for antisocial personality disorder is CORRUPT:

C—cannot follow the law
O—obligations ignored
R—remorselessness
R—recklessness
U—underhandedness
P—planning deficit
T—temper

No parent wants to think of his or her child as corrupt. Yet Scripture says that not one of us is blameless. We have all "sinned and fallen short of the glory of God" (Romans 3:23).

For many of us, it's hard to understand how our once-sweet little Johnny [or Susie] could be content to live as he does, or to hurt us, the parents who love him so deeply.

Judi Braddy knows all too well that sad experience.

After a particularly bad period of drug usage, her son came face-to-face with some personal demon and became afraid. He was scared and crying when he begged them to "just get me out of here." And so she and her husband came to the rescue:

> After spending most of the night calling one rehabilitation hospital after another only to be told that unless we had the right insurance—which we didn't—they couldn't help us, my husband finally found a treatment center two hours away in Reno, Nevada, that agreed to let us make payments. Just before dawn we loaded our son in the car and drove off.[2]

A few weeks later they were faced with a painful reality:

> Less than three weeks later he checked himself out of the program, and moved in with his girlfriend. Imagine our shock to also find out that our son and a buddy he had met in the program had been secretly doing drugs most of the time they

were there. It took us three years to pay off his three-week "treatment," a bill amounting to over $10,000.[3]

Like so many of us, Judi was seeing the son she remembered—the son she prayed would return—and not the manipulative person he had become. How easy it is to see what we want to see and ignore the facts staring us in the face.

My son had been home from the hospital two days when I knocked on the door of the RV. A self-contained fifth wheel we had set up next to our garage, it was the perfect size for one person and would accommodate my son until he could get on his feet, find a job, save some money, and get his own place.

We believed him when he said he wanted to make a fresh start. At least we wanted to believe him. Kevin and I had been married less than two years when we sat down together and established a list of rules and regulations, a contract as it were, that my son had reluctantly agreed to follow when he arrived.

"What choice do I have?" he'd asked.

He had been living on the streets, under bridges, in and out of homeless shelters, and having hit bottom (again), he was ready to start fresh, or so he said. What he didn't say was that he was also going cold turkey from a heroin addiction.

"Christopher, are you there?" I called out again, this time louder, as I continued knocking on the door of the RV. No answer, so I tried the door; it was locked. I went back inside our home for the extra key.

It was daylight, but inside the RV, it was dark as night. My son had covered all of the windows with blankets and towels. The smell of cigarette smoke assaulted me first, followed by the smell of fear. Something was very wrong; I sensed it.

My son was curled up in a fetal ball, drenched in sweat, shivering violently.

"You gotta help me, Mom," he cried. "It hurts so bad."

"What did you take?" I shouted. "Should I call an ambulance?"

"No! No ambulance." He spat the words. "I didn't take anything.

I stopped; that's the problem," he shouted, followed by a string of expletives not directed at me but at the unseen monster of withdrawal that held his body and mind captive.

I got him out of the RV, into my car, and to the emergency room on my own, crying all the way, fearing for his life.

"We can't draw his blood, and we can't get an IV into him, Mrs. Bottke," the nurse said. "He doesn't have any veins."

"What do you mean he doesn't have any veins?" I stared at the nurse who wouldn't look me in the eye. "Tell me what you mean," I asked calmly.

"His veins are all collapsed. It's typical of hard-core drug users. We've called a surgeon; he'll be down as soon as he can. We're going to try to get a shunt into a vein under his clavicle. It's our best shot."

I looked down at the creature who lay on the gurney in the emergency room—for it was not my son. Spewing vile language one moment and apologizing the next, shaking, crying, and screaming. He should have been in a drug-treatment facility, not in an RV in our backyard. But I just didn't realize...

And yet he hadn't gotten this way overnight. How could I have been so blind?

Frantic calls, pulling money from various accounts, buying basics like underclothes and toiletries, we managed to find a residential treatment facility in Minneapolis that had a bed available.

"At last he'll get the help he needs," I cried to my husband.

How quickly I had forgotten all the previous treatment centers I'd funded and helped him find over the years, starting in his teen years.

So what do you think is going to be so different this time? a tiny voice that I refused to acknowledge whispered in my ear.

In less than a week, my son was thrown out of the program for not following the rules—the no-fighting rule to be exact.

"I had to stand up for myself; you don't understand," he said staunchly. "He started it, but I had to finish it. It's the law of the jungle."

Except it wasn't a jungle. It wasn't the streets. It wasn't jail. It was his chance to get help, to start fresh.

But he clearly wasn't ready to get help. It hadn't really been his choice to begin with. I had done all the work. I had prepared the RV for him, paid for the costly emergency-room visit, then located the treatment facility and drove him to it.

"Honey, he doesn't want to change," my husband said. "Stop seeing what you want to see and start looking at who he really is. Allison, the plain truth is that you want a life for him that he doesn't want for himself."

When I got over being angry with my husband for being truthful, I began to look at my son differently. I began to see him as he really was and not how I wanted him to be.

How foolish I had been! It wasn't my battle! The battle belonged to the Lord, and it was time I handed it over to Him—all of it—once and for all. No matter how much I loved my son, now that I could see him for who he was, I had to distance myself from him.

> None of us wants to believe that our little angel is capable of being a bad kid, or on their way to being a bad adult. So we put up with their actions of using tears and manipulation, not because they are being hurt, but because we are afraid to be hurt by possibly losing their friendship for a time. Rest assured, they will be back, and grateful that you didn't cave in. As hard as it might be for us to believe, if we are using tough love on our kids, it's much easier on them than what someone else will do to them without love, so if we teach them, we will spare them a lot of future agony.
>
> —RON DICIANNI, ARTIST AND AUTHOR

Scripture is full of admonitions to separate ourselves from people who act in destructive ways. One of the most descriptive is in 1 Corinthians 5:1-13. Although the apostle Paul began by talking primarily about the sexual immorality among the people of Corinth, the lesson is clear that "a little yeast works through the whole batch of dough" (verse 6). And verse 11 is particularly explicit in its directive for believers to keep distanced from yeast—aka *sin:* "You must not associate with anyone who calls himself a brother but is sexually immoral or greedy, an idolater or a slanderer, a drunkard or a swindler. With such a man do not even eat."

Wow, that's tough love. And as hard as it is, many of us are taking a stand, fighting and binding up the wounds.

Countless parents refuse to believe that their children are involved in dangerous behaviors, that they may have a character disorder.

Although it's too late for prevention, it's never too late for redemption. Our only refuge is in God's grace and mercy. Restoration and blessing will come after judgment and repentance. Though the devil may seem to have won a skirmish or two, the battle is still the Lord's.

It's time now for you to take this critical step of taking off those blinders of wishful thinking or of happy childhood memories. It's time for you to see your child as he really is...not as who you wish he was.

5

The Power of Love and Forgiveness

She forgot her keys when she rushed out earlier that day, slamming the door after their heated argument. Now, Jennifer Cavalleri, played by actress Ali MacGraw, sat weeping on the doorstep, looking into the eyes of her beloved Oliver Barrett IV, played by Ryan O'Neal, and uttering the words that would find their way into the vernacular of an entire culture: *"Love means never having to say you're sorry."*

Years later, many of us from that generation have learned the hard way how untrue those words are. On the contrary, living a life of love, joy, and peace has everything to do with being able to say we're sorry.

I was a teenager when *Love Story* hit the movie theaters, quickly shooting to number one at the box office, sending a subtle message to society of no accountability.

As an adult, I now understand on a conscious level what the script-writers intended with this catchy hook—at least I'd like to think I do. And I'm not afraid to admit that *Love Story* falls in my top-ten list of all-time favorite chick flicks. Nonetheless, saying "I'm sorry" is one of the most powerful choices we can make when it comes to parental love. Asking forgiveness when we've been wrong is what repentance, reconciliation, and redemption are all about. And though it may sound strange to parents in pain, the decision to forgive is an important step in the process of gaining back your life. Parents in pain aren't the only ones who have discovered the power of healing in forgiveness. So vital is the act of asking forgiveness that it's step 8 of the AA 12-Step program: "Made a list of all persons we had harmed, and became willing to make amends to them all."

In her book *Ready? Set? Go!* Judy Hampton devotes an entire chapter to forgiveness. She writes,

> This is not the time to be a rights defender; it's time to be a truth seeker. If you have been falsely accused, God will be your defender. It's amazing, though, how God is honored when we own our own sin and ask forgiveness, but to genuinely forgive someone means asking for it. Author Philip Yancey calls forgiveness "an unnatural act." Our flesh would rather rise up and defend! But without forgiveness, our wounds will simply never heal. Sure, it's easier to nurture the pain. But if we want our wounds to start healing we must forgive. Forgiveness is an act of our will.[1]

In making the necessary choice to stop enabling my son and to set boundaries, I've found it necessary to look at five areas of forgiveness:

1. Forgiving those who have hurt us
2. Forgiving our adult children
3. Forgiving ourselves
4. Asking forgiveness from God
5. Asking forgiveness from our adult children

Forgiving Those Who Have Hurt Us

In *Seven Prayers That Will Change Your Life Forever*, Stormie Omartian listed one prayer as the "prayer of release." She begins by sharing her painful past as the often-abused daughter of a mentally ill mother. It's easy to see how her mother's behavior left Stormie with feelings of futility, hopelessness, helplessness, and deep emotional pain. Struggling for years with issues that frequently had their roots in the polluted soil of her childhood, Stormie spent decades looking for love in all the wrong places, filling the empty places in her heart and soul with empty promises and pursuits. How well I could relate! Confessing her sins and asking the Lord into her heart entirely changed her life, but it wasn't until Stormie could forgive her mother that real healing began. Stormie's Christian counselor said:

> You don't have to feel forgiveness in order to say you forgive someone. Forgiveness is something you do out of obedience to the Lord because He has forgiven you. You have to be able to say, "God, I confess hatred for my mother, and I ask your forgiveness. I forgive her for everything she did to me. I forgive her for not loving me, and I release her into your hands."[2]

In this short book, Stormie goes on to talk about the power of forgiveness and the pain of unforgiveness. As children of God, we know when we repent that we are forgiven. Yet the process of becoming all God intends us to be isn't achieved with that one salvation prayer.

Like Stormie, many of us have pain in our past that must be forgiven—on many levels. We need to forgive people who have harmed us, confess any unacknowledged sin, and ask forgiveness of people we have harmed, purposely or not. Only then can we experience the freedom to truly live as God intended—free of bondage from guilt, blame, shame, and a host of other feelings that have played out in countless ways over the years.

"The most important thing to remember when it comes to forgiving is that forgiveness doesn't make the other person right, it makes you free. The best way to turn anger, bitterness, hatred, and resentment for someone into love is to pray for that person. God softens your heart when you do and brings wholeness into your life,"[3] wrote Stormie.

Listen to these Bible verses on forgiveness:

Therefore, my brothers, I want you to know that through Jesus the forgiveness of sins is proclaimed to you. (Acts 13:38)

In [Christ] we have redemption through his blood, the forgiveness of sins, in accordance with the riches of God's grace. (Ephesians 1:7)

The Bible is filled with countless lessons on forgiveness, like those I just mentioned, and yet I know how difficult this step can be.

Some of you may say, "Okay, I get what you're saying, Allison, but I dealt with all that stuff years ago, I don't want to dredge it all up again. Been there, done that."

Amen to that! I know exactly what you mean. Praise God if you've already visited the places in your heart and soul that needed repair, asking and giving forgiveness in all areas, including forgiving yourself. There is no need to relive the sins of our past over and over. Once forgiven, always forgiven—that is the power of God's love for us.

However, looking at forgiveness in conjunction with our enabling and how it relates to healing is a decidedly different perspective, requiring a new thought process and skill set.

Forgiving Our Adult Children

When it comes to forgiving our adult children, we have two very specific issues going on simultaneously. On one hand, we may be angry with our adult children, and rightfully so in many cases. We may even harbor more than a little resentment and righteous indignation over how they have treated us. Many of our adult children have lied to us, stolen from us, disrespected, used, and abused us. They've forgotten or ignored our birthdays and most major family holidays. They've caused significant money problems in many of our lives, as well as a loss of respect in our communities and, in some instances, in our churches. Many of us have suffered great damage to our marriages, and some of us have even divorced because of the strife. Our relationships with friends and family have been damaged. Some of our adult children have used us as pawns in their games of illegal activity. We don't trust them, we can't believe them, and many of us don't even know them anymore, so far off the deep end have they gone.

Add on top of this the anger we feel at what they are doing to their own lives. The red-hot pain we feel when we see the loss of potential, the wasted lives, and the opportunities they had to change but never did. The list goes on and on.

As we begin to distance ourselves emotionally from the situation and begin to look more objectively at the reality of what has happened, we are filled with mixed emotions—most of them negative—directed squarely at our adult children who have made such poor choices.

We must forgive them for what they have done to us, even if they don't ask us for forgiveness. God's Word says, "Forgive, and you will be forgiven" (Luke 6:37). As Stormie Omartian writes,

> That verse also says that we shouldn't judge if we don't want to be judged ourselves. Instead, we are to release people and circumstances to God and let him be the judge. When we forgive people who have hurt us, we restore their God-given worth and value—not because they deserve it but because God has already done the same for us,[4]

Judy Hampton knows how difficult this step may be for us. She writes,

> Does the very thought of making things right with your prodigal adult child make you angry? Maybe you haven't done anything wrong in your eyes. Maybe all you've done is help. Yet you've been met with false accusations, disdain, blame, and rejection. Perhaps you think your prodigal should be asking you for forgiveness! I understand. When someone has taken your heart out and stomped on it, it's difficult to imagine you need to forgive. I can't count the number of parents I've met with horror stories. Parents who have been physically abused and subjected to cruelty, revenge, and unbelievable manipulation. But the point is, if we do

not forgive our prodigal, then it will affect us in a negative way. If we don't forgive, what we are saying is, "God, my child is more important to me than a healthy relationship with you."[5]

Forgiving Ourselves

Along with forgiving our adult children, the second simultaneous issue is the guilt we feel over the part we have played in this drama.

Guilt is a good thing. Without guilt we have no inner barometer telling us we may have done wrong, we may have made a mistake. Remember the list of APD character traits? If you recall, a lack of guilt or conscience played a significant part in many of the traits. We need to *feel*—to *know*—that we have done wrong. Yet we cannot wallow in guilt, shame, and blame, allowing it to color everything in our lives with huge brushstrokes of gray, covering truth in a murky film, keeping us distanced from God, who wants so much more for us and from us.

During the years I wandered lost in the desert of disbelief, I made more than a few bad choices. Some I knew at the time were wrong. Others I justified as acceptable because the "world" had preached tolerance, and I bought the lies. Things like living with my boyfriend before we were married, engaging in premarital sex, and even considering abortion a viable alternative. I often felt as though I coined the term *serial monogamy,* as I had several live-in fiancés over the years, and I justified the cohabitation because, after all, we were eventually going to be married. But somehow we never were. My lifestyle was filled with partying, drugs, alcohol, and the if-it-feels-good-do-it mentality so prevalent in the 1970s and '80s.

I raised my son in a less-than-ideal environment, yet I felt strongly that I was being a good mother because I loved him so much and worked hard to keep a roof over his head and give him the things I never had as a child. Today I know now that I lived a selfish, sin-filled life, yet at the time I justified a great many of my lifestyle choices as the right ones.

When I look back now, it's hard to believe I'm talking about myself. Today there is little doubt in my mind that God had a plan for my life even when I didn't acknowledge His existence.

Asking Forgiveness from God

If there's a downside to making a U-turn toward God as an adult, it's the initial period of intense pain a person goes through when he or she becomes convicted of sin. Because I was unfamiliar with God's truth, as written in His Word, I had no idea how sinful a life I had been living. The more I read the Bible and the more I understood sin, salvation, redemption, and restoration, the more I cried out to God to forgive me. I had so much to be forgiven for.

Back in my very early days as a new Christian, I clung to a Bible verse that assured me I was on a new course in my life: "Therefore, if anyone is in Christ, he is a new creation; the old has gone, the new has come!" (2 Corinthians 5:17).

Countless Scripture verses guided my path on my new journey, filling me with hope and healing and taking away my guilt and shame over the choices I had made. Understanding true repentance and forgiveness of sin was difficult for me because there were so many layers to peel back.

We ask God to forgive our sin, cleanse our hearts, and make us new. We say, "I'm sorry, God, for all the wrong I've done. Please change my life and give me new direction." Receiving God's forgiveness is a major step, letting the reality of what He has done for us fully penetrate our hearts and souls.

Forgiveness on so many levels is key, and then we must move on and not live in the past.

Asking Forgiveness from Our Adult Children

Uh-oh. This is a really tough one. Why should I ask my child to forgive me? Shouldn't it be the other way around? In her response to my questionnaire, author Jill Rigby, who has a great deal of experience working with parents in pain wrote:

In working with parents of troubled adult children, I've found that parents who refuse to accept their responsibility for the mess their kids are in can't receive healing and can't help their children heal. Repentance of the parents is a key in beginning the healing process. The self-esteem movement has told us that any troubles we experience must be due to someone else…that we are all victims, rather than face the truth that there are always consequences of our choices…good and bad. Accepting responsibility is always the beginning of restoration. Accepting God's forgiveness for our misguided parenting and then looking an adult child in the eye and asking for their forgiveness is powerful.

This crucial step of asking the forgiveness of your adult child, though very hard, may be the healing balm needed to prepare him or her for an enhanced growth spurt. Then again, it could be like pouring lighter fluid on an open flame. You won't know until you try.

In *Boundaries,* Henry Cloud and John Townsend have devoted a section to forgiveness and reconciliation. What they say in the chapter "Resistance to Boundaries" is pivotal to gaining SANITY:

Many people have a problem determining the difference between forgiveness and reconciliation. They fail to deal with external resistance because they feel that they have to give in to the other person again and again or they are not being forgiving. In fact, many people are afraid to forgive [or ask forgiveness] because they equate that with letting down their boundaries one more time and giving the other person the power to hurt them again.

The Bible is clear about two principles: (1) We always need to forgive, but (2) we don't always achieve reconciliation. Forgiveness is something that we do in our hearts; we release someone from a debt that they owe us. We write off the person's debt, and she no longer owes us. We no longer condemn her. She is clean. Only one party is needed for forgiveness: me. The person who owes me a debt does not have to ask my forgiveness. It is a work of grace in my heart.

This brings us to the second principle: we do not always receive reconciliation. God forgave the world, but the whole world is not reconciled to him. Although he may have forgiven all people, all people have not owned their sin and appropriated his forgiveness. That would be reconciliation. Forgiveness takes one; reconciliation takes two.

We do not open ourselves up to the other party until we have seen that she has truly owned her part of the problem. So many times Scripture talks about keeping boundaries with someone until she owns what she has done and produces "fruit in keeping with repentance" (Matt. 3:8). True repentance is much more than saying "I'm sorry"; it is changing direction.[6]

Therefore, simply telling our adult children that they are forgiven doesn't mean reconciliation will occur in our relationship. As I said, our children may not even be ready to admit they've done anything wrong. Conversely, when we confess our sins to our adult children, we cannot have a preconceived plan for how this will turn out. As Cloud and Townsend write, it's more than saying we are sorry; we must change our direction. For enabling parents, that change in direction is bound to bring more than a bit of resistance from our adult children. Yet this is where it starts.

Let me caution you: Don't turn this apology into a full-blown argument. The goal is not to fill your adult child with fear and dread over what kind of plan you have up your sleeve. Be careful not to get into a discussion over past behaviors. You can memorize what you'd like to say or read it from a script. You may also choose to write your apology in a letter in the event verbal communication is all but impossible, which is so often the case in situations like this.

You do not want to blame your adult child for anything, no matter how much at fault he may have been. Finger-pointing will serve no purpose at this juncture.

The fact is, you are the parent, and you've made some poor enabling choices, and now that is going to stop. First, however, you need to set things right with God and your adult child. Following is a sample script that may guide you as you ask for forgiveness from your adult child:

> I (we) need to say something to you that isn't easy for me to say. I know we've had our share of arguments over the years, and I've said some pretty harsh things to you. I'm sorry for that. I've been frustrated with the situation for a long time. Nothing I do seems to work, and when things do change, it doesn't take long until we're right back where we started. It's like we're on a merry-go-round that never stops.
>
> I've been blaming you for a lot of the anger and pain I feel, but it's not your fault how I choose to feel. My choices are my responsibility just as your choices are your responsibility.
>
> Over the years I've made some poor parenting choices. I want to apologize for that. I've begun to realize that in choosing to accept responsibility for your actions and choices, I have robbed you of valuable life lessons. I have stunted your growth as an adult. I want to take this time to apologize for the part I played in making you overly dependent on me and ask you to forgive me for any pain I may have caused you in the past.
>
> I want you to know that I've learned some new things I believe will help us get off the merry-go-round—things I intend to share with you soon.
>
> I know some of the changes I'm going to begin implementing are going to be difficult for you to understand at first. It may seem like I don't care or that I've abandoned you. But that isn't true. I want you to know I love you and believe in you. I want what is best for both of us. We both deserve lives of peace, joy, happiness, and success.
>
> Please know that my intentions are not meant to cause you harm or pain. My prayer is that you will begin to make positive choices and fully accept the consequences of your actions, and in doing so, that you will reach a level of

self-respect that will empower you to be all God created you to be. I love you and I believe in you. I pray for you to believe in yourself.

I'm sorry, and I'm asking you to forgive me for any part I have played in causing you pain.

Saying this to your adult child isn't going to be easy, but you must do it. This redemptive work will pave the way for true healing to begin. Our desire as parents is to respond to our children with love. For many of us, that has been all but impossible to do for quite some time. The anger and animosity run deep.

However, the season of change is now upon us.

Part Two

The Six Steps to SANITY

Let's say we're diagnosed with a severe illness: Sickness X.

Sickness X is a serious illness, to be sure, yet it can be cured by following a prescription that includes taking medicine and changing some specific habits. We trust our physician to know what he's doing, so we get the prescription filled, begin taking the medicine, and follow the doctor's orders so we'll get better. Some medications are short-term, some are long-term, and others are for life. Some medicines have a bitter taste; others have no taste. Many have side effects; others do not.

But if the medicine will cure us, we will gladly suffer the bitterness, the side effects, and even endure the long road to recovery. We know that treatment is better than leaving the disease in its present state.

Consider the Six Steps to SANITY, outlined in the following chapters, our medication to help cure our illness of enabling. One dose won't do it; we'll need to stay on this prescription for quite some time until we return to full health. Just as our adult children may slip back and forth into their dependency on us, so too we may slip back and forth into our habit of coming to their rescue.

However, we must pray for the strength to remain firm in our resolve to make changes. Backsliding at this point is very dangerous, as we will lose not only our credibility with our adult children but any momentum we may have gained as a result of the changes we are making. Therefore, we must continue on this prescribed course of "medication" for the duration of the treatment—no matter how difficult it may be.

I must caution you, however, that there is a possibility of a long-term side effect in following this course of treatment. In time we will begin to regain our SANITY, and we will begin to feel a sense of self-respect and peace despite any crisis.

What is SANITY? This is what we gain when we stop focusing on our adult children and begin to focus on changing our own attitudes and behaviors.

How do we get SANITY? By recognizing and identifying the false conceptions we have about ourselves and our adult children and replacing worldly lies with spiritually empowering truths.

In what situations will SANITY work? We can implement the six steps to help an adult child grow up who

- has never left home;
- has returned home (with or without mate/children);
- considers our home a revolving door;
- lives on his or her own (or with others/roommates); or
- is a full- or part-time college student.

I trust by now that you've begun to realize the part you have played in this ongoing drama of enabling, as well as the enemy's tactics in using these negative feelings against you. I pray that you have realized the futility of harboring the negative feelings of guilt, frustration, anger, fear, and inadequacy and that you are ready to develop new strengths to begin living a life of freedom from bondage. It's time for healing—emotionally, spiritually, financially, and psychologically.

Here then are my six steps to SANITY:

Six Steps to SANITY

S = STOP your own negative behavior (especially the flow of money!)

A = ASSEMBLE a support group

N = NIP excuses in the bud

I = IMPLEMENT rules and boundaries

T = TRUST your instincts

Y = YIELD everything to God ("let go and let God")

Last but not least, another side effect of implementing the Six Steps to SANITY could be that our adult children may actually become the people we've been pretending they were or dreaming they could be! Now wouldn't that make all the tough-love pain worthwhile?

6

Step One in Gaining SANITY:

STOP Your Own Negative Behavior

"I'm so glad you're still open," the woman said, heading for my garage. "I saw your sign this morning, but I was on my way to work and couldn't stop. Then I had a job interview. Do you have any baby clothes? I'm looking for my daughter; she's having another baby next month."

In my Midwest town, and all over the country I would imagine, a seasonal celebration is the spring garage sale or yard sale. Along with cleaning out the clutter, the high point of these community events is meeting new folks and visiting with old friends who stop by—getting a taste of the amazing difference in humanity.

I didn't have any baby clothes, but after visiting with "Edna" for close to an hour, I wanted to rush out and buy some for her. (Apparently my enabling includes strangers as well.)

During our chat, I found out that Edna worked three jobs, one full time and two part time. The job interview she'd had that day was for a third part-time job.

People are starved for someone to listen to them, and listen I did as Edna began to collect items from my garage sale, placing them on the picnic table where I sat, and told me how much her daughter could use such-and-such an item for her house.

"I sure hope I get the job," she confided. "I need it to help my daughter pay for her car. She bought a new SUV last year, and she can't make the payments now."

Edna told me her daughter was a stay-at-home mom with two children and a third on the way.

Now I'm the first to admit I'm not a very shy person, and I probably overstep my boundaries from time to time (okay, often), but this is a matter near and dear to my heart. I had to know more about Edna's situation. Why was she responsible for making her daughter's car payments? How long had this been going on? I looked at Edna's car, a late-model Ford in reasonably good condition from what I could see, yet far from new.

"How many hours a day do you work now?" I inquired.

She rattled off her schedule. "About 15 hours on Mondays, Wednesdays, and Fridays. Tuesdays and Thursdays are short days at only 10 hours each, and on weekends I only work 5 hours each day. That's why I'm looking for another part-time job on weekends in the afternoons."

My heart ached. This woman worked seven days a week. Why did her daughter need a new SUV that I was told cost almost $500 per month in bank payments—not counting gas, insurance, and maintenance? I thought back to my first car when my son had been a baby: a sturdy, used Dodge Polaris bought at a police auction. Sure, times had changed, but when did parents start feeling responsible for supplying their adult children with vehicles better than their own, and at the cost of their own health? How long could a woman in what I presumed to be her late 50s keep up this grueling schedule?

Did her daughter even care?

Apparently this adult child couldn't afford to live in the lifestyle she currently enjoyed without her mother's help.

Perhaps the saddest part of all is that Edna didn't seem to recognize this enabling lifestyle for what it was: a crippler of both her and her adult child.

But once we all *do* finally recognize our negative behavior for what it is—and how damaging it's become—we won't be able to just pick up where things left off. God willing, we will feel a deep conviction in our souls to make changes, to stop our enabling behavior.

One of the critical first things we must immediately stop is the flow of money to our adult children. We must stop being the First Bank of Mom and Dad or the Community Bank of Grandpa and Grandma.

Don't misunderstand, I'm not advising you to put down this book and march up to your adult child, declaring, "That's it! The gravy train stops right now!"

Yes, the flow of money must stop, but unless your adult child has been told to leave your home immediately, this severance of financial dependency must be carefully planned by you and your spouse and any other enablers in the equation: grandparents, siblings, aunts, well-meaning friends.

No matter how angry we may be, no matter how broken our hearts, we must act in love. Our goal is to release and empower our adult children, not to cause them even more pain than this change in our behavior will most certainly cause. Therefore, stopping the flow of money is not the only thing that must be carefully planned.

Remember, although it is our prayer that our adult children will become healthy, independent, and responsible members of society, just because we develop a plan and present it to them, doesn't guarantee that they will joyfully embrace the change or even recognize it for the opportunity it is. What they do with their lives as a result of our implemented boundaries will be their choice.

Our primary goal is not to stop their negative behavior or to stop their drug or alcohol abuse or to stop their lying, cheating, stealing, or the never-ending chain of excuses we've grown accustomed to hearing and they've grown accustomed to delivering. Of course, we'd love for all those things to stop, but it's up to them to change their lives, their behaviors, their habits.

Our primary goal is to stop *our* negative behaviors, gain SANITY in our own lives and if we're married, in our life as a couple. We must carefully plan these action steps as well.

Based on my experience and the feedback I received from psychologists and counselors, there are twelve critical Stop Steps we must take to forever end the insanity and turn our lives around. While all twelve steps are important, the top four are critical. We must

1. *Stop* repeating negative enabling behavior in all its forms

2. *Stop* ignoring our own personal issues

3. *Stop* being alone in our pain

4. *Stop* the flow of money

1. Stop Repeating Negative Enabling Behavior in All Its Forms

Talk is cheap. It's one thing to say we'll stop enabling our adult children, but when it comes to matters involving both the heart and the head, it's a decision that must be made with a great deal of prayer and discussion, not with our adult children but with our spouses or support-group accountability partners. We must be fully convinced of the need to stop repeating our negative enabling behaviors. We must be ready, willing, and able to give the process of change our total commitment. We must be prepared for the inevitable storms that will come. We'll stand strong only if our initial commitment to stop was thoroughly thought out and fully committed to.

In her book *The Emotionally Destructive Relationship,* Leslie Vernick addressed the truth about change and how it begins when we stop.

> I hope you see by now how lying to yourself is so detrimental to your well-being. When we habitually deceive ourselves we cannot grow or mature in a godly way. As painful as truth can be, we must face it if we want to become healthy, no matter how much we don't like what it tells us.
>
> Recently a woman named Linda e-mailed me. She wrote:
>
> I believe that getting out of a destructive situation has nothing to do with recognizing that the other person is abusive and/or that we are not safe, or in getting the other person

> to change. I believe that I began to change when I realized
> that my life was spiraling downward and I felt hopeless. I
> realized that the choices I'd made over and over again were
> not getting me closer to joy but were taking me further and
> further down a destructive road. Recovery came for me when
> *I decided that I needed to change,* and that I'm the only person
> I could affect or change, and that I couldn't do this alone.
> I needed God.[1]

The most painful step in any healing process is often the first one.
You must face the ugly truth that you're in a destructive relationship
and that you are the one who has allowed it to continue. Just like
a person wouldn't begin chemotherapy unless she first accepts that
she has cancer, you will not take the steps necessary to grow, heal, or
change if you are still in denial. As long as you minimize the truth
about your problem, you cannot become strong enough to challenge
or change anything. Wherever you are, it is important you realize that
stopping the destructive dance starts with you.

2. Stop Ignoring Our Own Personal Issues

It wasn't until I checked myself into a one-month treatment program to sort out the mess I had made of my own life that I began to
see my enabling behaviors for what they were.

There are so many extenuating circumstances involved in why we
do the things we do, and so many intricate components in how we've
arrived at this place in life. However, in my experience there appears
to be a common theme in the overall pathology of enabling parents:
the general neglect of our own hearts. Whether it's a relatively minor
issue that needs to be addressed or a major malady, the fact is that we
tend to focus so much time and energy on the problems of our adult
children, we have neglected the issues that have made us who we are
today. We must be willing to look at ourselves to identify our reasons
for allowing things to get so out of hand. We cannot begin to implement the changes that need to occur if we aren't willing to recognize
the parts we play in the drama.

Have we really thought through some of the reasons why we've made ourselves so available to our adult children? Some of the reasons may include the following:

- guilt over perceived failures as a parent (and the feeling that we must somehow compensate for our past failures)

- the sad (and somewhat perverse) need to be appreciated by our adult children. (Buying our children's love by enabling their lifestyles only perpetuates both our problem and theirs.)

- influencing our children against their other parent. (Again, a perverse issue, but it does exist.)

- some aspect of our own upbringing that is influencing us to enable our children. (Were we deprived of love or physical needs in our youth, and are we compensating by giving our children what we never had?)

- lack of trust in God for the outcome if we cut off the flow of money to our adult children. (At some point, every Christian parent of an adult child will have to release that child to God and *learn* to trust Him for whatever happens.)

There are no doubt many other possible reasons you may need to acknowledge. Think about it. Pray about it. What issues must you deal with in your own life at this time?

3. Stop Being Alone in Our Pain

For too long we've felt like outcasts in a world of perfect parents and perfect kids, when in reality, families just like ours are all around us. Parents in pain exist in our church homes, in our workplaces, and in our neighborhoods—and they are often suffering in silence. Support groups such as Al-Anon and Co-Dependents Anonymous meet in locations around the country. Joining, or in some cases starting, a support group is vital. Professional therapy is often the best way to go when we need to make significant changes in our lives. Having the benefit of an objective opinion and the therapeutic advice of a professional is invaluable. In addition to professional counseling on an hourly or sliding-scale basis, many resources are available to us at little or no cost. We may have to do a bit of research to find them, but it will be worth it. For many of us, it's much too difficult to heal without objective, qualified, and nonjudgmental help. The "A" in the Six Steps to SANITY will further address this issue.

4. Stop the Flow of Money

It doesn't matter whether we are on a fixed income or are blessed with abundant financial resources, a common denominator among enablers is the flow of money to our adult children. It doesn't matter whether it's $20 or $20,000, we must stop coming to the rescue with our checkbooks. Our money must cease being the life preservers that buoy up our adult children, keeping them afloat through yet another storm. We might be amazed at just how well our adult children can swim when given the opportunity to do so. More important, they just might be surprised at their own ability to survive without life support, a powerful lesson that no amount of money can purchase. Judy Hampton says, "The day we stopped the flow of money was the day we realized that all the money we were giving our adult children was only underwriting sin and addiction."

Change STARTS When We STOP

These four Stop Steps are critical to our healing, but there are numerous other Stop Steps we must consider along the journey.

We need emotional distance from our situation to gain a better perspective and obtain objective insight. Therefore, we must immediately stop engaging in arguments or negotiations of any kind. Period. We must stop feeling guilty, angry, used, and abused. However, if your adult child is threatening actual physical abuse, do not hesitate to take drastic measures to ensure your safety, including calling the police. It's a sad and painful thing to recognize that some sociopathic adult children are extremely dangerous. There are documented cases of adult children taking the lives of others as well as the lives of their parents. Be aware of your own adult child's proclivity to violence if he is provoked, and prepare accordingly.

This first step in the Six Steps to SANITY will be one of the most difficult. They say the first step in any journey of growth is difficult, but without this crucial first step, we'll never arrive at our destination. However, what exactly is our destination? About this we must be clear.

What Are Your Goals?

In preparing to develop your action plan, make a detailed list of all your life goals and the ultimate destination you wish to reach in your lifetime. There is no right or wrong answer to this exercise. This is your chance to dream on paper. Everyone must do this individually, and if you're married, you must also do this as a couple, making sure your ideas of a destination are compatible.

For example, if my goal in life is to raise cattle on a ranch in Wyoming, and my husband's goal is to make a killing on Wall Street and live in a plush condo near Central Park, then I'd say we have a bit of a problem, a failure to communicate, as it were. However, it isn't unusual for a married couple to get out of sync in their ultimate destination as husband and wife when the focus has been too long on an adult child. That's why it's so vital that we begin to communicate openly, without reservation. We must understand that not only are we presenting our adult children with a new paradigm, but as a couple we are also entering a new stage in our marriages. Our roles as parents of adult children are going to change, starting now. And we may need to correspondingly adjust our goals as single adults or as married couples.

Remember the oft-quoted definition of *insanity:* repeating the same behavior and expecting different results.

Now is the time to stop repeating the behavior that hasn't produced the desired results. Now is the time to change course. It's time to stop destructive behaviors and patterns and start charting a firm and focused course that will get you—and your spouse—to your ultimate destination.

If in the course of your new journey, your adult child manages to find his way as well, this will be an answer to prayer. And although there is no guarantee that your new choices will be embraced by your adult child, you still need to make them for your own peace of mind.

As a reminder of the STOP measures you'll need to employ, photo-copy this expanded STOP list and put it in a place where you'll see it often—the refrigerator door, a bulletin board, the bedroom mirror, or some other prominent place:

Step 1 to SANITY: Stop

THINGS TO STOP, STARTING NOW

1. Stop repeating negative enabling behavior in all its forms
2. Stop ignoring my own personal issues
3. Stop being alone in our pain
4. Stop the flow of money—now
5. Stop pretending things are going to be fine if I continue as I have been
6. Stop putting off the changes that must be made
7. Stop my own destructive patterns and behaviors
8. Stop feeling guilty
9. Stop demanding that my adult child change
10. Stop making excuses for his or her negative behaviors and/ or choices
11. Stop engaging in arguments, debates, or negotiations—no verbal volleyball
12. Stop being a martyr

Step Two in Gaining SANITY:

ASSEMBLE a Support Group

As the first step of *stopping* our enabling behavior is being implemented, enjoying the support of others is crucial. Parents in pain need support, understanding, encouragement, and accountability from others who have traveled this painful journey and come out on the other side—*or* those who are currently walking the journey with us. Some of us may also need a willing individual to intercede on our behalf during times of crisis.

Traditionally, when we think of support groups, we think of well-known groups such as Alcoholics Anonymous (AA) or Al-Anon or other 12-step programs. But for many parents, drugs or alcohol aren't part of the problem. Such groups would be inappropriate for them. But the good news is that support groups come in all sizes and varieties. They don't have to center around substance abuse.

It's true, our adult children fall into many categories. Some of us have adult children with drug and alcohol problems, yet some may not be chemically dependent. Others have adult children dealing with addictions to gambling or pornography. Some adult children may have a debilitating sense of entitlement that will take great strength to change. Additionally, the financial duress our adult children may be under, along with us, could quite possibly be at astronomical levels, leading to strained finances or even bankruptcy.

Some of our adult children may be living with us and others are not. Some are in jail or prison. Many of us have adult children in college (either living at home or on campus), and we are beginning to see a dangerous pattern of poor grades, extensive partying, and growing irresponsibility. Some of us have irresponsible adult children who are parents themselves and often leave us to care for their children—our grandchildren—part time or full time.

Some of our adult children have no desire to work, and others are trying hard to be successful. Some wouldn't consider asking us for money but have become dependent on our continued support in other ways, such as babysitting, doing laundry, or helping with homework. Others owe us anywhere from $50 to $50,000 and some have come to depend on (or feel entitled to) our ongoing financial support as if it were a weekly paycheck. We have adult children who want us to cosign on loans for cars, education, home furnishings, even houses. Some of us are dealing with adult children who are in their 20s, while others are wrestling with adult children in their 30s, 40s, or beyond.

And as painful as it may be to admit, some of us have adult children whose character traits match those described earlier as characteristics of antisocial personality disorder. These adult children are most likely going to need professional counseling and ongoing, long-term therapy to make changes in their lives. Some may be a danger to themselves or to us, and still others may need extended stays in residential treatment programs or psychiatric facilities.

The Common Denominator

While there is no common denominator for categorizing the issues our adult children have, we must remember our primary goal: we are here to gain SANITY in our own lives, to recognize what it means to enable, and to *stop our behaviors* in relation to whatever issues our adult children may have.

Therefore, any group we may join or start up will represent varied circumstances among the parents involved, yet there will be one common denominator: us, the enabling parents. In this we are the same. Our adult children may fall into different categories, but in the enabling category, we are one.

That's why we need the help of a support group.

AA works because it's one alcoholic helping another. A support group for enabling parents will also work for the same reason; it's one parent in pain helping another. Sharing resources, stories, techniques, and strength—not giving advice.

Nowhere in Scripture is the importance of traveling the road together more beautifully depicted than in Ecclesiastes 4:9-12:

> Two are better than one,
>   because they have a good return for their work:
> If one falls down,
>   his friend can help him up.
> But pity the man who falls
>   and has no one to help him up!
> Also, if two lie down together, they will keep warm.
>   But how can one keep warm alone?
> Though one may be overpowered,
>   two can defend themselves.
> A cord of three strands is not quickly broken.

We need others around us in good times and bad. It is during times of trial and tribulation when fellow brothers and sisters can lend life-changing support and encouragement by listening, praying, and offering a shoulder to lean on.

Support-Group Options

It doesn't matter which type of support group you become involved in. It only matters that you get involved. Listening to others share their perspectives and pain allows us to gain objectivity, something many of us lack. Being able to let it all hang out in a safe and nonjudgmental environment can be both healing and empowering. Five support-group options include the following:

- Self-help support groups
- Professionally run support groups
- Online support groups
- Codependent support groups
- Six-Step SANITY support groups

Self-help support groups are fully organized and managed by members, usually volunteers. Alcoholics Anonymous (AA), Co-Dependents Anonymous (CoDA), and various other 12-step programs, typically facilitated by members, are examples of one major type of self-help group that is also sometimes referred to as a fellowship, a peer support group, a mutual help group, or a mutual-aid self-help group. This is where Six-Step SANITY support groups fall. (*Note:* to find out where a Six-Step SANITY support group may be meeting in your neighborhood, or for guidelines on how to begin your own Six-Step SANITY home support group, log on to www.SanitySupport.com.)

Professionally run support groups are facilitated by a professional, such as a social worker, a psychologist, or a clergyperson. The facilitator controls discussions and provides other managerial services. Such professionally run groups are more often found in institutional settings, including hospitals, drug-treatment centers, and correctional facilities. There may or may not be a fee involved to attend this type of group.

Online support groups have been around since at least 1982. Diverse remote networking formats have allowed the development of both synchronous groups, in which individuals can exchange messages in real time, and asynchronous groups, in which members who aren't connected to a network at the same time can read and exchange messages. E-mail, Usenet, Internet bulletin boards, chat rooms, and blogs have become popular methods of communication for self-help groups and among facilitated support groups.

Support groups have long offered companionship and information for people coping with diseases or disabilities, but online, situationally oriented groups have expanded to offer support for people facing various life circumstances, especially those involving relationships. The wide range of support groups now active on the Internet can offer individuals support for an equally wide range of life circumstances. It isn't difficult to find an online support group, but it may be hard to find the right one.

Codependent support groups, most typically, Co-Dependents Anonymous (CoDA) is a 12-step program founded in 1986 in Phoenix, Arizona. Members strive for healthy relationships and to overcome codependency. There are about 1,200 groups in the United States, and others internationally.

A self-identifying statement for CoDA reads as follows:

> Most of us have been searching for ways to overcome the dilemmas of the conflicts in our relationships and our childhoods. Many of us were raised in families where addictions existed—some of us were not. In either case, we have found in each of our lives that codependence is a most deeply rooted compulsive behavior and that it is born out of our sometimes moderately, sometimes extremely dysfunctional family systems [as in enabling]. We have each experienced in our own ways the painful trauma of the emptiness of our childhood and relationships throughout our lives.[1]

As for all 12-step groups, the third tradition identifies the membership requirement. In the case of CoDA it reads, "The only requirement for membership in CoDA is a desire for healthy and loving relationships."[2]

Although there are fewer CoDA support groups, they are popping up with alarming regularity around the country. Since many enabling parents share codependency traits, I strongly recommend this support group.

Six-Step SANITY support groups are another option in the event you don't have easy access to an existing support system, or should current support groups not quite meet your needs. I would encourage you to consider assembling a Six-Step SANITY support group in your community, based on the principles set forth in this book. Our membership requirement mirrors that of CoDA—"to build healthy and loving relationships"—and much like AA groups, Six-Step SANITY support groups encourage anonymity and nondenominational affiliation.

Overcoming Silent Shame

Many parents in pain have grown accustomed to maintaining a kind of silent shame about sharing the circumstances and issues surrounding their adult children. Attending or assembling a support group is the last thing we want to do.

Yet it's one of the first things we must do to gain strength in a season of life that will most certainly require every ounce of fortitude we can muster. At times when our strength runs low, we must have others willing to intervene on our behalf and hold us up. We must begin looking at our circumstances objectively, emotionally distancing ourselves from our situations in order to gain a healthy perspective.

Making clear choices based on facts, not feelings, will be critical as we move ahead. The best way to do this is through prayer and group support.

8

Step Three in Gaining SANITY:

NIP Excuses in the Bud

When we make the decision to resign from the role of enabler in our children's dramas, the story line, as many of us know from experience, can quickly turn to melodrama. Face it, many of our children have continued so long in their present situations because they've been very good at manipulation. It's difficult sometimes for us to accept this ugly fact. We want so much to believe them when they tell us what turns out to be a lie, or a rather overdramatized truth.

Have you ever heard any of these lines from your adult child?

- "I'm just too tired!"
- "But mom, things are different today!"
- "You just don't understand."
- "I'll start on Monday. I promise."
- "Things will be different this time."
- "It's not my fault!"

You will no longer accept those excuses—and many others just like them. This is the third of the Six Steps back to SANITY: nip excuses in the bud. Make it evident early on that you have no intention of being swayed by clichés or con games or lame excuses.

Real healing begins when a parent stops believing the excuses and lies and insists on the truth. As we develop our action plan, there must be no room for excuses. Our boundaries must be firm. There is a right and there is a wrong, and we are going to choose to do what's right. Period.

How is it—why is it—so many adult children don't seem to know right from wrong? How is it that we as parents sometimes don't seem to know the difference either?

As I travel the country sharing my U-turn testimony from New Age secular humanism to Christianity, I often use the phrase "I was so open-minded, my brain slipped out."

This comment always brings a wave of laughter from the audience, yet I pray the deeper meaning isn't lost. During my years as a nonbeliever, I bought the worldly lie that virtually everything was acceptable, that my response in a given situation depended solely on how I viewed the situation or on extenuating circumstances. I had raised my level of tolerance for all things to an art form.

Alas, this dangerous mind-set has become frighteningly prevalent in our culture.

Even those who are not noted for their evangelical faith have realized this. FOX TV correspondent and journalist Bill O'Reilly has become a tireless warrior spotlighting this shift in our culture. In his bestselling book *Culture Warrior,* he writes,

> The traditional culture warrior understands that a clear definition of right and wrong is imperative for a disciplined society that protects its citizenry. One of the outrages of modern America is the secular-progressive philosophy of confronting harmful behavior by providing a variety of excuses for it. For example, the "abuse excuse," whereby criminals become objects of sympathy because they, themselves, were abused, has taken deep root in the United States.... We are now seeing the most repulsive acts, like the rape of children, being "understood." Instead of harsh punishment for child abusers, some judges are opting for lenient sentences and the

option of "treatment" for felons who destroy kids. This is the most egregious example I can provide of secular-progressive "justice."

Mr. O'Reilly continues:

> By contrast, the traditional culture warrior believes in the Judeo-Christian code of forgiveness—but with punishment and with penance. True justice demands that punishment fit the crime. We in America must continue to uphold the standards of behavior that protect people, especially children and the elderly, from harm. Civilized conduct is not "relative." In the American republic, the people decide what acts are wrong (illegal), and those acts must be punished accordingly. That code of justice, historically based upon Judeo-Christian principles, is one the secular-progressives would tear down. Traditional warriors must prevent that from ever happening.[1]

Although Mr. O'Reilly's book focuses on the "culture war," I feel strongly that as enabling parents in pain, we are in a war as well, with Satan as our enemy. We have believed many of the worldly lies referenced throughout *Culture Warrior,* and the similarities to the enabling epidemic were more than obvious to me as I read this provocative book.

Just as Americans must take responsibility for what has happened in our national culture, so too must parents take responsibility for what has happened in our families. In raising our children, too many of us bought into too many worldly lies, and we have reaped the harvest of excuse after excuse after excuse from our adult children.

After years and years of enabling, I was getting older and wiser—but not wise enough. The subtle ways I continued to enable were becoming clearer to me, but it took a comment from my son to shake me into a reality I had never before experienced—a reality that forever removed the blinders from my eyes, giving me an empowered strength of purpose.

Being a writer isn't just what I do for a living; it's more than a "job." For me, and I would guess, for many writers, it's the way we communicate best. That's why I decided to write as I sat in the courtroom awaiting my son's SWAT-raid arraignment hearing.

What began as a random train of thought turned into a letter to my son—a letter that would go undelivered.

> Dear Son,
>
> We haven't spoken since your arrest. Today is your arraignment hearing. You are not yet here. There are two men wearing jail jumpsuits sitting in the courtroom, along with a uniformed police officer. I recognize them from their photos in the newspaper; these two men were arrested with you on New Year's Day.
>
> The court reporter is the daughter of a close family friend—how ironic. Yet this is a small town, and as you know, Kevin's profession brings him in contact with a great many people.
>
> I am sick—at heart, stomach, and mind, but not at soul. This will not break me. I will not let Satan take me down. I will not let him win. I will continue to pray for your safety and for your salvation.
>
> I know you say that you are saved, yet your actions don't match your words.
>
> You had a chance at a new life this time. You had freedom—unfettered freedom—for the first time in a long time. You no longer had to look over your shoulder; your record was clear at last, enabling you to start over fresh. You were renting a nice home with a garage and space enough for your home-based business. Things were looking up for you! What happened?
>
> An officer has just walked you into the courtroom. You are in handcuffs. I looked you in the eye, and you looked down after shaking your head. Was it in shame? Or in distress that you were caught? I don't know what you must be feeling—anger, frustration, remorse, or...what?

I wonder, do you even feel? Is your heart hardened?

Do you know how those of us who love you feel? This pain in my heart aches like a festering wound. I look at you sitting there in leg chains and handcuffs, wearing an orange jumpsuit. Your head is shaved almost bald. Is this part of the neo-Nazi lifestyle? You've repeatedly denied the Nazi association for years; have I been blind?

It's quiet in the courtroom. The judge took a 15-minute break, waiting for your arrival. Another uniformed officer has walked into the courtroom—also a family friend. In fact, he and his wife recently had dinner in our home and joined us at the country Christmas concert at our church over the holidays. He was surprised to see me in the courtroom.

"That's my son," I whispered, nodding toward you. Nothing more was said. What else could be said? For all I know, he was part of the huge SWAT raid that took place at your home on New Year's Day. The day you were arrested. I have a copy of the search warrant and a list of 38 items of evidence taken from your home. It's public record.

I read it through tears when it was handed to me.

How is it that tear ducts do not dry up? How can tears come when a heart is wrung dry?

Today we'll find out when your hearing will be held and if the judge will grant you bail.

My letter stopped there when the judge returned. And in short order a long list of charges was read, my son was assigned a public defender, a court date was set, and he was given a $10,000 bail, of which 10 percent would be needed for him to leave jail that day.

A stranger tapped me on the shoulder.

"I'm your son's bail bondsman."

My son had his own bail bondsman. How convenient.

"If you can pay the $1,000, we'll have him out of here in no time."

"No."

"No?"

"That's correct."

He looked at me as though I'd grown a third eye on my forehead and retreated, shaking his head at my son, who scowled.

The tears came again. I tried to hold them back, swallowing hard, quickly wiping my already puffy eyes with a handkerchief. My pain was so great, expressed in a seemingly nonstop flow of tears.

I was weary from weeping.

My son then managed on his own to come up with the money and with someone to guarantee the $10,000 bail in the event he didn't show up at his hearing. He was out of jail by that afternoon, spouting a list of excuses for what he called a "bogus bust."

He returned to his ravaged home, where he became incensed that I had removed some of his belongings and dumped out all his liquor.

Yet it was his collection of German paraphernalia that concerned him most when at last he called.

"Some folks collect Precious Moments statues; I collect war memorabilia. What's the difference?" he told me, demanding back the items I had removed from his home. I found it difficult picturing a delicate little porcelain statue of a sweet, wide-eyed child in the same league as a cabinet filled with Nazi swastikas and weapons used to annihilate millions of people.

Later that same day I dropped off the offensive collection at his home, and he wouldn't come to the door, sending instead his on-again, off-again girlfriend to help remove the bags and boxes from my car.

A few days later I was on the phone with a close friend who had talked to my son.

"He said you refused to help him get out of jail."

"That's right, I did."

"Is it true that it was only $1,000?"

Only? Clearly she didn't understand.

"It's not about the money anymore," I said. "I can't keep doing this."

Once again the tears came. I was so bone-tired from the tears, pain, anguish, and fear for his life.

"His landlord evicted him," my friend continued. "He has to move; it's stressing him out. He says they haven't got a case. There weren't any drugs in the house."

I wasn't about to get into an argument with my friend; she had no idea of the long list of items the SWAT team had removed from his home. She didn't understand how many times I had sat in a courtroom listening to charges brought against my son. She had no conception of the pain I felt every time I saw my only child in handcuffs and leg chains—or the feeling of talking to him on a prison phone through thick, plate-glass panels. She hadn't experienced the never-ending list of excuses.

Then came the pivotal situation that helped remove the blinders from my eyes—the final step in my freedom from bondage.

"Allison, he said you put on quite a show in the courtroom. That you cried so everyone would feel sorry for you."

I've never been stabbed, but I imagine the pain I felt in my heart at that moment was close to it.

"What?" I stammered.

"He said you were crying so people would feel sorry for you."

I got off the phone as quickly as possible before my friend could discern that I was crying once again, this time going from anguish to anger as her words sank in.

He thought I was crying to gain sympathy?

Clearly my son was unaware of the depth of my pain, and therefore, I also assumed, the depth of my love for him. All the years I had come to his rescue out of love for him—out of a desire to keep him safe, to help during his trials and tribulations—all for naught. He didn't get it. He *never* got it. Not only didn't he get it, but he didn't appreciate it. Not only didn't he appreciate it, but I suddenly realized with crystal clarity that instead of helping him, my actions had hindered him. He had no idea how to feel remorse, empathy, or shame. In fact, I feared he had no idea how to feel at all, and I doubted he knew his behavior was wrong.

Gaining this new level of understanding was like a blind man receiving his sight. The remembrance of the raw pain that had coursed through my weary body in that courtroom came back in waves as I weighed the reality of my feelings with my son's twisted perception of them.

Sympathy? Dear Lord, help me understand this.

I'd stopped the flow of money long before, yet I was still supplying my son with "things" that cost me money, so in reality I hadn't stopped the flow of money at all. I was still listening to his never-ending litany of excuses for his circumstances, wanting so much to believe. I had showed up yet again in a courtroom to lend my support, to offer my unconditional love, to show him that no matter what he did, I still loved him and would be there for him.

The time had come to stop being there for him—at least in this way.

I needed to adopt a different response to my son's choices. It was time to nip his excuses in the bud, as well as my own excuses for continuing to enable, no matter how subtle. No more would I lay my heart on the chopping block of his uncaring life. It was time for a new set of boundaries, with geographic distance being a key factor.

My son was a fallen human, yet so was I. I had fallen back into old habits of enabling, subtle yet nonetheless negative and damaging. No longer would I accept the excuses. It was time to go back to the drawing board and revamp the action plan I had developed years earlier, starting with revised boundaries.

Lord, I prayed, *I don't want to harden my heart, but I desire instead to protect it. Please help me to love my son in a way that is also loving to myself. I can't take this pain anymore. Enough is enough. Please once again heal my broken heart.*

Bill O'Reilly says,

> At times you have to fight. No way around it. At some point, every one of us is confronted with danger or injustice. How we choose to combat that challenge is often life-defining.

You can face difficulties head-on, or run from them, or ignore them until they consume you. But no one escapes conflict. No one.[2]

I was ready for the conflict and the consequences.
I was ready to draw the line in the sand.
Are you?

9

Step Four in Gaining SANITY:

IMPLEMENT Rules and Boundaries

In our modern culture, boundaries get a bad rap. In reality, appropriate boundaries are *good*. In the Bible, God set boundaries for His children. And He set consequences for when those boundaries were violated. God loves us...but He does give us boundaries for our behavior that are for our own good. When we violate His boundaries, He still loves us, but we suffer not only from the natural consequences of violating those boundaries but also from a loss of fellowship with Him (though not a loss of relationship).

A parent's unconditional love for his or her child does not mean looking the other way when that child exhibits negative behavior and makes poor choices. Establishing a clear set of rules and boundaries is vital when the goal is to heal the hurt our enabling has caused. As Pastor Bill Oudemolen from the Foothills Bible Church in Littleton, Colorado, says,

> Many twenty-first-century parents have chickened out on establishing parameters for their kids (e.g., rules), the main thing kids really want (and need) from parents. Boundaries bring security. Lack of boundaries breeds insecurity. In my role as pastor, some of the most troubled adults I see were

raised in permissive environments. And…logically, some of the most secure knew clearly every boundary their parents had—whether they agreed with it or not.

Boundaries provide not just a sense of security, but they also define, in a valuable way, the parameters of who and what we are. In his book *Epic,* John Eldredge makes note of the very large maps we so often find in malls, amusement parks, and hospitals—the ones that indicate our exact location with a famous red star and the words *You are here:* "These maps are offered to visitors as ways to orient themselves to the situation, get some perspective on things."[1]

We all need those sorts of markers in our lives—not just our adult children, but us as well. We all need to know where we are at any given time. In the same book, Eldredge refers to our lives as an "Epic Story." I like that analogy:

> We can discover *the* Story. Maybe not with perfect clarity, maybe not in the detail that you would like, but in greater clarity than most of us now have, and that would be worth the price of admission. I mean, to have some clarity would be gold right now. Wouldn't it?[2]

You can say that again! Gold? There have been times in this journey with my son when I would have settled for silver, even copper—anything that was a step up from the lump of black coal I felt best represented the story of my life.

In her book *Listen,* author and speaker Keri Wyatt Kent encourages readers to find God in the story of our lives. This book is filled with valuable information for strengthening our relationship with God, and the wisdom the author imparts within its pages found its way into my heart as it relates to enabling our adult children. In her chapter "What Is My Desire?" she writes,

> Lately, I've also felt freedom in places where I have said no, as in, no, I can't do that for you; no, I am not going to be responsible for your feelings; no, I am not going to rescue

you from the consequences of your own irresponsible behavior; no, I am not going to arrange my life around trying to maintain an image of perfection. I'm finding freedom, that is, in setting boundaries.[3]

As I read Keri's words, I found myself being buoyed up, strengthened. For parents in pain, reality tends to be one crisis after another. Pain, heartache, agony, stress, pressure, and emotional turmoil we've got, but freedom? Not by a long shot.

Yet freedom can be found, and hope and healing are possible as surely as morning comes after night. Joy and happiness can eventually be found as well. Perhaps not right away. Perhaps the pain you now feel will increase before it decreases. Although I can't predict what will happen when you make the decision to change *your behavior* toward your adult child, I *can* predict what will happen if you don't: things will get worse before they get better.

In my research for this book, I found countless resources to help parents learn to establish effective boundaries for young children and guidance to help mold the minor-age toddlers, youth, and teens still living at home. Hands down, it is in the formative years of our children's lives that parents have that brief window of opportunity to raise emotionally and spiritually healthy humans.

Jill Rigby's book *Raising Respectful Children in a Disrespectful World* is one of the best I've read, and *The Mom I Want to Be—Rising Above Your Past to Give Your Kids a Great Future* by T. Suzanne Eller is another epic resource. Both books are firmly rooted in solid biblical principles and firsthand experience from the trenches of life. If you have minor-age children at home, no matter their age, I recommend these valuable books.

Alas, the resources available for those of us who missed this window of opportunity, for whatever reasons, are rare. When it comes to learning how to handle the convoluted circumstances of overdependent adult children, the guidance is scarce. Many of us are winging it through the murky waters of trial and error by the skin of our teeth.

Emily Post was right on the money when she wrote, "Any child can be taught to be beautifully behaved with no effort greater than quiet patience and perseverance, whereas to break bad habits once they are acquired is a Herculean task."

Herculean, yes; impossible, no. As Christians, we do have a great promise in Philippians 4:13: "I can do everything through [Christ] who gives me strength."

In the hundreds of questionnaires I distributed for this book, more than one person shared the classic study that was conducted with children who had or did not have boundaries.

Grade-school children were told to go out to play in a school yard that had no fence. They wound up staying very near the building, afraid they might wander too far away. In contrast, another group was sent out to play in a school yard that had a fence. That group played all the way to the fence and even on it. They knew how far to go.

Our adult children have no idea how far they can go because we have been either noncommittal or inconsistent regarding our boundaries.

We've been sending mixed messages for years about what is acceptable and what isn't, what we'll tolerate and what we won't. We've perfected the boy-who-cried-wolf syndrome by not establishing and sticking with firm boundaries and consequences.

In their book *Boundaries* Henry Cloud and John Townsend clearly describe how God intended us to handle this dynamic of helping:

> We are responsible *to* others and *for* ourselves.

This is a key principle for us to learn in developing new behaviors.

> "Carry each other's burdens," says Galatians 6:2, "and in this way you will fulfill the law of Christ." This verse shows our responsibility *to* one another.

It's the *to* and *for* difference that has tripped many of us up.

> Many times others have "burdens" that are too big to bear.

They do not have enough strength, resources, or knowledge to carry the load, and they need help. Denying ourselves to do for others what they *cannot* do for themselves is showing the sacrificial love of Christ. This is what Christ did for us. He did what we could not do for ourselves; he saved us. This is being responsible "to."

Remember the distinction between *helping* and *enabling* back in chapter 1? The good doctors go on to clarify this further:

> On the other hand, verse 5 [in Galatians 6] says that "each one should carry his own load." Everyone has responsibilities that only he or she can carry. These things are our own particular "load" that we need to take daily responsibility for and work out. No one can do certain things *for* us. We have to take ownership of certain aspects of life that are our own "load."[4]

We've been carrying too many loads. We've confused the *to* and the *for*. It's time to stop. Implementing acceptable boundaries is not an option; it's a requirement.

However, where do we begin?

Detach

One of the keys to changing the reality of our situation is the ability to detach ourselves from it. Detachment from someone else's problems is a key tenet in AA. Their literature says,

> Detachment is neither kind nor unkind. It does not imply judgment or condemnation of the person or situation from which we are detaching. It is simply a means that allows us to separate ourselves from the adverse effects that another person's choices can have upon our lives.

When I heard that my son thought my courthouse tears were intended to solicit sympathy, I had a gut-wrenching moment of revelation. I realized the time had come for me to physically remove myself from his life for a season. As painful as it would be, I could not continue to be around him. *I had to detach physically as well as emotionally.*

Many parents in pain find that they have become more obsessed with their adult child's behavior than their adult child is with his own behavior. We want our adult children to change more than they want to change, or more than they even think they need to change. The Al-Anon program teaches family members of alcoholics to "put the focus on ourselves" and not on the alcoholic or anyone else. The same holds true for enabling parents. If we put the focus on ourselves, we will no longer be in a position to

- suffer because of the actions and reactions of others;
- be used or abused by others;
- do for others what they could do for themselves;
- cover up for anyone's mistakes or misdeeds;
- create a crisis;
- prevent a crisis if it is the natural course of events; or
- manipulate situations so our adult children will eat, sleep, get up, pay bills, and not suffer the consequences of their choices or actions (i.e., take care of their business for them).

In my weakness I could suddenly see what I needed to do.

Listen

Keri Wyatt Kent says that often we must listen from a place of weakness: "Good listeners have clear boundaries. They are not emotional repositories for everyone else's problems."

Ouch. I realized that is what I had become.

Keri goes on to say, "This is no easy line to tread. So, how can we listen lovingly but still maintain boundaries?"[5]

As parents in pain, we've been living in places of weakness for a very long time, but we haven't done the kind of listening that has brought us closer to God—or to any firm results in the challenges of our lives. We have become emotional repositories for everyone else's problems, and the time has come for that to stop. We must learn to listen with love within the framework of healthy boundaries.

Keri continues:

> We all have seasons in certain friendships where we give more than we take. But is it a pattern in most of your friendships? Do you listen but not really speak truth to friends who may need it? Do you feel that people take advantage of you? Do you resent being taken advantage of but then slide quickly into feeling guilty about your resentment? Do you think it's "Christian" to always put others first?
>
> It may be that you have a problem with setting boundaries, so you are listening from a place of weakness.
>
> Loving listeners listen from a place of strength. They don't take on responsibility for things that are not their fault. They don't allow people to manipulate or blame or shirk responsibility.[6]

Define Boundaries

If we truly want to be "loving listeners," we must become strong. Implementing rules and boundaries is a major part of acquiring the strength we're going to need on the journey.

In the course of my experience, I have learned several "must" truths about defining boundaries with adult children:

- We must have a clearly defined action plan before confronting our adult children.
- We must establish consequences and stick with them.
- We must present a unified front if we are married.
- We must not get involved in debate, discussion, or trying to help our adult children figure things out.

- We must encourage our adult children to figure things out for themselves.

- We must be willing to ask ourselves, "Who am I outside of this issue/child?"

- We must be willing to shift the focus off our adult children's lives and onto our own.

In a little book that packs a powerful punch, best-selling author Cecil Murphey has written an empowering collection of daily encouragement messages titled *When Someone You Love Abuses Drugs or Alcohol*. Each bite-sized entry is food for the soul, and the short prayer that follows every message is sweet surrender. Although not everyone is dealing with the addiction component, I find Mr. Murphey's advice nonetheless beneficial:

> I've been in the Church since infancy. Yet I never recall a leader telling me, "You're doing too much." Instead, I was always told to give more, to do more.
>
> Sermons reminded us of Christ's unsearchable gift of life and how much God gives to us. We had countless examples of selfless givers and dozens of Bible verses to prod us on. We didn't examine our motives, believing that the needs determined the action. I envisioned myself as the Good Samaritan, who found the half-dead traveler on the road and nursed him back to health.
>
> I've finally learned that caretaking doesn't work, in the Church or in the home. I wasn't nursing people back to health—I was teaching them dependence. I helped prevent them from learning to fend for themselves.
>
> *Merciful God, forgive me for trying to ease pain by making people dependent on me.*[7]

Reading this encouraged me in three ways. I realized that

1. I was not alone;

2. even good Christians fail; and

3. I could take my situation to God in prayer.

In developing our action plan, we'll look at defining and establishing boundaries with our adult children, as well as identifying firm consequences, in the following areas:

- communication
- living arrangements
- finances
- employment
- family
- education

In the event our adult children did not have healthy (or consistent) boundaries as kids, it's never too late to begin establishing them now. What they choose to do with the new parameters is going to be up to them. Our number-one priority is to remain firm in our resolve.

It's never too late to implement rules and boundaries, to make choices that will change our lives. God *can* transform our relationships with our adult children.

10

Step Five in Gaining SANITY:

TRUST Your Instincts

It's amazing to me that so many of us parents make decisions about our adult children that are in direct opposition to our gut feelings, our parental instincts.

Dozens of parents in pain who responded to my questionnaire berated themselves for not paying more attention to their instincts. One anonymous mother had a particularly bad experience:

> My son drove a new car and had two, not one but two, fancy motorcycles. He had a good job selling office equipment, but I knew he wasn't making enough money to afford those things. He had all kinds of reasons for the stuff he brought home: "a friend gave me this cool MP3 player" or "I got a great deal on the cycle; I couldn't pass it up" or "I'm just storing the 42-inch flat-panel TV here until my buddy moves," and on and on the stories went. I was such a sap to believe him, and what makes me even angrier is that I had a feeling something wasn't right. I felt in my gut that something was wrong.
>
> He was arrested for dealing drugs. When the police searched our home, they found a floor safe under the carpet in his

room containing cash, jewelry, cocaine, and methamphet-amine. He'd installed a floor safe in our home without our knowledge! It cost us considerable legal fees to clear our own names, as we faced charges of being accessories. Although it was embarrassing to admit that we had been duped in such a way, it was more of a nightmare to think we might actually have to suffer the consequences of not following our instincts. Thankfully, we were exonerated, but our son is serving an extended sentence in a federal prison. He has placed our names on the list of visitors he refuses to see.

Did this happen overnight? Did young Johnny wake up one day and decide to deal drugs, using his parents' home as a storehouse for his stash? Highly unlikely.

Intuition is a powerful tool. However, that still small voice will eventually stop talking altogether if we continue to ignore it.

Parents often know in their gut when things aren't right—when that inner voice speaks to their hearts about specific situations or issues. Yet we repeatedly ignore the voice and negate our instincts. One parent wrote, "I saw the signs…late nights, sleeping in, irritability, weight loss, that 'look' in his eyes. I just didn't want to admit that my son had a serious problem."

Nowhere does the need to trust our instincts hold truer than when we suspect our adult children are on drugs, have alcohol problems, or are involved in illegal activity. It's like a sixth-sense alarm goes off in our hearts and souls, shrilling a warning to take heed. A warning many of us have ignored for too long.

When I was a girl, I loved to watch the TV program *Lost in Space*. The Robinson family had such amazing adventures. For years afterward, anytime I felt in my gut that trouble was imminent, I would hear the warning phrase of the robot echoing in my mind: "Danger, Will Robinson! Danger, Will Robinson!"

Oh, that we had our own flailing-armed robot to shout words of warning to us concerning our adult children!

Our inability to trust our adult children has us questioning our ability to trust our own instincts. In fact, the erosion of trust on many levels often has us acting out in ways that show little resemblance to God's plan for our lives.

Trust is a key issue in our faith.

We may not trust our adult children—or even ourselves at times—but we need to trust that God is always in control. We also need to trust that He can speak to us through our parental instincts.

Back when I was a new Christian, I was given a copy of *The Bible Promise Book,* a paperback filled with Scripture listed under alphabetical categories ranging from "Anger" to the "Word of God." I've gone through numerous copies of this powerful little paperback over the years, since it leads me to Scripture based on the issues I'm experiencing. Under the topic "Trust"[1] are nine separate verses, including Proverbs 3:5-6:

> Trust in the LORD with all your heart
> and lean not on your own understanding;
> in all your ways acknowledge him,
> and he will make your paths straight.

If we trust in the Lord with all our hearts, we must also trust what He teaches us about the power of the Holy Spirit:

> I will ask the Father, and he will give you another Counselor to be with you forever—the Spirit of truth. The world cannot accept him, because it neither sees him nor knows him. But you know him, for he lives with you and will be in you. (John 14:16-17)

I'm not a theologian, and I'm sure there are countless reference materials available on the amazing power of the Holy Spirit. However, in my experience I've found this one thing to be true: when I am walking in God's will for my life, I can clearly feel the power of the Holy Spirit within me, and this often manifests itself in very distinct impressions of how I should respond, behave, and think. It's as though my instinct is a divine power guiding me to do what is right.

Now, lest you think I have an inside track on discernment, let me assure you that this powerful guidance is available to each and every one of us who believes in Jesus. Although I've never heard audible words shouting in my head, "Hey, Allison, don't believe a word he's saying," I have felt distinct impressions over the years that I have both acted on and ignored. And without a doubt, the times I ignored that still small inner voice, I ended up kicking myself in the backside, saying something akin to this: "I'm so mad at myself! I knew at the time he was lying. I knew I shouldn't have said such-and-such or done such-and-such. Why didn't I listen to my instincts?"

That's a good question—why don't we? Well, maybe one reason is that we know that if we acknowledge what our intuition is telling us, we must then address the problem. But if we ignore what our intuition is telling us, we can ignore the problem. Pretend it isn't so. Or perhaps it's just our imagination.

When we listen to our instincts, we are challenged to do something, even if that something is to do nothing. Therefore, it's much easier to simply not listen at all—to ignore what in our hearts we know is true. Hiding our heads in the sand is the only way some of us have managed to survive at all. And for many of us, the reality is, quite frankly, very frightening. Especially when drugs and alcohol are involved, as they so often are—whether or not we're ready to admit it.

One of the most difficult things to understand when we are dealing with adult children who have issues with drugs or alcohol or exhibit any of the APD traits listed earlier is the fact that for the most part we can't believe what our children say. All the more reason to trust our intuition.

It may seem hard to think that way, especially for Christians who are taught that love "believes all things" (1 Corinthians 13:7 NKJV) and that we're to forgive and help our adult children at all costs. We want so badly to believe our adult children, to give them the benefit of the doubt. But a time must come when we step back and look at the facts without emotion and recognize and identify the problem for what it is.

In our guts we know something is rotten in Denmark. Yet for

many of us, that's where we might as well be living, so distanced are we from accepting truth and reality. This is when having a support group is crucial. When we are in doubt about the validity of something concerning our adult children, it's more than beneficial to vocalize our suspicions with a supportive group of people we trust. Then we need to muster the courage to follow through on what we know we must do.

Of course, some parents are alarmists, seeing evil at every turn, fearful of much and expecting the worst in just about everyone and everything. Unjustly accusing our adult children of foul play can be as damaging as closing our eyes when we suspect something is wrong.

In responses to the questionnaire I distributed, two great confirming quotes I've found regarding our parental intuition are these:

> When it comes to stopping our enabling behavior, we must have courage. We must trust our instincts and best judgment. Both are gifts of God given to us to utilize in rearing our kids. (Rebekah Montgomery)

> Our instincts are God-given and can be trusted. When my two children were born, my mother said, "Honey, throw most of the books away. Your children come with instructions written on your heart." Many times we override God's message to our heart, and then we see the consequences. (Sue Buchanan)

Listen to your instincts.

Is something telling you that illegal behavior is occurring, including but not limited to such things as drug and alcohol abuse, drug dealing, theft, harboring fugitives, sexual immorality, and a host of other issues? Are things happening right under your roof that you feel powerless to stop? Is there a chance your grandchildren are being exposed to illegal and dangerous activity in their home?

Take back your power! Do something proactive. This is your home. This is your life.

Trust your instincts.

11

Step Six in Gaining SANITY:

YIELD Everything to God

In the hundreds of questionnaires people from around the country returned to me, the respondents were virtually in 100 percent agreement when it came to the necessity of yielding our situations with our adult children to God. Yet while everyone agreed that it was indeed a vital component, they equally agreed it was one of the most difficult aspects in actively applying faith to our daily walk.

For some parents perhaps, religious faith wasn't much of an issue when you brought up your child. It certainly wasn't on my radar screen when my son was small. But that's one thing about being a parent in pain; you realize that the help you need is going to have to come from some other source than yourself.

Having a dysfunctional child can sure put a parent on a steep learning curve. I had to learn from scratch what it meant to be a Christian, and what God's Word taught when it came to the worldly lies I believed for so long. For a long time I felt unable to set healthy boundaries for my adult child because I felt guilty, ashamed, and unworthy myself. I felt as if my many parental mistakes meant that my deserved punishment was to simply handle my pain (and its source—my son) myself. I wasn't sure about the idea of yielding my son and my pain to God.

And like many parents in pain, I was also hesitant to look at the role Satan was playing in the vicious scenario. For many of us, it's difficult to think of our adult children as pawns in Satan's diabolical game of life, yet that accurate visualization makes it all the more possible for us to boldly turn them over to the only One who can ultimately save them.

We've tried everything else.

We've tried to control our environments, our adult children, and our relationships with God as well. Some of us are regular churchgoers, some of us believe in God but not in attending church, and still others are "Chreasters," folks who attend church only on Christmas and Easter. Some of us, dare I say, have even bargained with God concerning our adult children along this line:

> I promise I'll be good, God. I'll read my Bible every day, go to church, be nicer to my spouse, whatever it takes—if you'll just make things better in the life of my child, get him out of trouble with the law, help him find a job, help me get the money to bail him out of jail. Please, God, help me figure out this mess! Okay, God? Thank you. Amen.

Rarely in our prayers do we think about listening to God or about implementing the biblical principles that will bring stability to our lives. Instead, we fall back on bargaining. But I've discovered that listening to what God teaches us in His Word about all things—parenting included—should be the number-one goal in the life of every Christian. Too often we listen instead to worldly advice, to secular self-help gurus, and to the never-ending stream of trendy cultural messages designed to fix whatever ails us. Ironically, those were often the very sources of "wisdom" that either caused us to make parenting mistakes *or* caused our children to succumb to temptations that led them into their destructive lifestyles.

We may listen to the way the world may view us with our trials and tribulations—as people to be pitied or shunned. When we believe this falsehood, we often become too weak to be of benefit to anyone, including ourselves.

T. Suzanne Eller had a difficult life, filled with one turbulent trial after another. Although Satan could easily have slipped in at any number of junctures, he could never gain a foothold in this courageous woman's life. She writes,

> Life circumstances become an excuse for a negative approach to life, marriage, and to parenting—if we let them. Allowing our perception to expand is one of the most powerful tools we have to unlock the mysteries of joy. You have within you the potential to continue to grow, to dream, to grasp the possibilities, and to savor the moments. When you do this, you begin to glimpse the many miracles of life—through the power of perspective.[1]

Suzanne views her life through the lens of her faith. She understands God's definition of life: that "while we are shaped by our past, we are not defined by it."[2] Repeatedly in her work, she returns to the truth that God is in control, that only when we let go and let God handle things can true healing and hope come from the ashes of despair.

I'm continually in awe of how God's Word can direct us if only we'll get out of our own way. Being in control of everyone and everything had been my safety net for years, keeping me from doing the work necessary to heal the deep wounds of my heart.

True Growth Requires Letting Go

Leslie Vernick is a licensed clinical social worker and the director of Christ-Centered Counseling for Individuals and Families. Day after day she experiences firsthand the devastating effects our past has on our present. Underlying virtually every issue is the mistake many of us make in hanging on tightly to the reins of our lives—or the lives of others. Leslie knows that true growth requires letting go. In her newest book, *The Emotionally Destructive Relationship,* she writes,

When we attempt to accomplish greater emotional and spiritual work, we usually think about all the things we need to *add* to our lives. We want to read and study the Bible, do meaningful ministry, gain greater emotional stability, better our interpersonal skills, or seek additional wisdom. All these endeavors can be helpful in our maturing process. But I have found in my own life as well as in my counseling practice that deeper and more lasting change usually comes about when we regularly practice letting go rather than doing more.

Recently I was speaking with Richard, a client, who feared God's judgment when he died because he wasn't working harder to do more. As we talked I said, "Perhaps we've gotten the concept of final judgment wrong. What if, in the end, Jesus isn't going to tell us everything we've ever done wrong or failed to do? What if he's going to show us the person we could have become and the things we would have done if only we allowed him to heal and mature us?"[3]

True healing begins when we make the head-heart connection that we must "let go and let God" concerning all things, not just the painful situations concerning our adult children. This kind of surrender doesn't mean we are giving up, that we no longer care what happens to our adult children. On the contrary, it means we relinquish their care to a far greater and infinitely more powerful Caregiver. It means at last that we have come to the end of our own selfishness and can now see the possibilities available when we step out of the way of spiritual progress. About this Leslie writes,

> Letting go in order to grow can be scary. It requires change, which demands a certain degree of faith and hope. That's why our picture of God must heal, at least a little, before we can embark on greater growth.
>
> The writer of Hebrews reminds us that we can only let go and run the race of life well when we keep our eyes on Jesus. Abiding and surrender...continue to be important as we practice the discipline of letting go.

There are three things we must learn to let go of if we want greater healing and maturity in our lives—we must let go of: unrealistic expectations, negative emotions, and lies.[4]

I wish I'd had Leslie's book years ago.

For so long I expected my son to live the kind of life I wished for him to live—a life he himself has no desire to live. Therefore, my expectations were unrealistic. I had to let go of those false (and unfair) expectations.

When the "letting go" part has been accomplished in our hearts and the "letting God" part becomes the focus of our lives, something amazing begins to happen: we feel free. We may not even realize how binding a prison our fears concerning our adult children had been until those fears are gone.

A mother who has had horrific experiences in this regard and has requested to remain anonymous said in her questionnaire,

> I'm discovering that it's okay to go ahead and have joy in my life. No matter what. Yielding everything to God, total surrender, is something I must do daily. I open my hands and release those I love to Him. I'm discovering His plan is so much better than mine, and I'm learning that I'm not God, like I used to think. I thought I always knew what was best for everybody in every situation. I'm learning to surrender my will in everything, including my will for those I love.

A husband and wife who have had a long and arduous journey on the road of enabling had this to say about the "Y" step in our Six Steps to SANITY:

> Nature is the best example we have for yielding everything to God. The birds and animals care for their young, and they instinctively know the right time to simply let them go. Regardless of what we may have done right or wrong in the past, the important thing is to understand that we did the best we could at the time, and now it's time to "let them go and let God."

Some of us may jokingly refer to ourselves as yielding "experts" since we have yielded our situations to God time after time, after having, of course, taken them back. As author Kathi Macias says in response to my survey,

> Yielding to the Lord is something I do well—time and time again—and then I "unyield" just as quickly, sometimes without even realizing it. I think if I had one thing to say to parents with adult children in this situation, it's that the points mentioned throughout this book must be worked through many, many times—perhaps for life. And that's a tough thing to accept. But just like our adult children who so easily slide back into their dysfunctional behaviors, so do we enablers slide back into helping them stay dysfunctional.

In reference to yielding everything to God, dozens of questionnaire respondents mentioned Paul's admonishment in the letter to the Ephesians to be alert and persistent and to put on the armor of God.

> Finally, be strong in the Lord and in his mighty power. Put on the full armor of God so that you can take your stand against the devil's schemes. For our struggle is not against flesh and blood, but against the rulers, against the authorities, against the powers of this dark world and against the spiritual forces of evil in the heavenly realms. Therefore put on the full armor of God, so that when the day of evil comes, you may be able to stand your ground, and after you have done everything, to stand. Stand firm then, with the belt of truth buckled around your waist, with the breastplate of righteousness in place, and with your feet fitted with the readiness that comes from the gospel of peace. In addition to all this, take up the shield of faith, with which you can extinguish all the flaming arrows of the evil one. Take the helmet of salvation and the sword of the Spirit, which is the word of God. And pray in the Spirit on all occasions with all kinds of prayers and requests. With this in mind, be alert and always keep on praying for all the saints. (Ephesians 6:10-18)

I still find it hard to understand how and why it took me so long to get on with my own life. How could I have all this head knowledge about the dangers of enabling, yet have a heart that continued to exist in a world all its own? I know many of you feel the same way. But we must resist the urge to continually blame or berate ourselves for what we have no ability to change. The past is the past! We must get on with our lives.

As a teenage mother, my entrance into parenthood was fraught with trial and tribulation, and my son's story is woven intricately into mine. As someone who speaks publicly about my own U-turn journey toward God, I'm often asked about my son and how he is doing. Over the years many fellow sisters and brothers have come alongside me to pray for him.

When the topic of this book became public, people from around the country began to send encouraging and supportive e-mails, sharing their own painful stories. It was as though in removing my finger from the dam, I had set free a torrent of tears from others who were walking the same road with me.

One of those fellow sojourners is Judy Hampton. Her books *Under the Circumstances* and *Ready? Set? Go!* also minister to parents in pain. Judy sent me this e-mail shortly after the SWAT-team raid on my son's home:

> Let's pray together that God gets ahold of our sons' lives and dramatically changes them. I can say this, Allison…being on the other side. The day you really give your son to the Lord…you will find life without that gut-wrenching pain again. There is really nothing *we* can do to change them… and when you just give 'em to God, life takes on a whole new meaning. Trust me, it's a process of surrender. We will not be involved in our sons' lives until they own their stuff and decide to get help. We've tried to make that happen countless times. They have to want it. It is what it is. God is able…more than able to handle our sons. It's the cross we must pick up daily to follow Him. May God use your pain as a platform to comfort others.

Judy included this Scripture passage with her uplifting message:

> Praise be to the God and Father of our Lord Jesus Christ, the Father of compassion and the God of all comfort, who comforts us in all our troubles, so that we can comfort those in any trouble with the comfort we ourselves have received from God. For just as the sufferings of Christ flow over into our lives, so also through Christ our comfort overflows. (2 Corinthians 1:3-5)

Judy understands, as do many parents and grandparents in pain, what it's like to live in the middle of insanity: "I know your agonizing pain and guilt...broken heart, humiliation, discouragement, and destitution of spirit. Moms hemorrhage inside at the heartache of having a prodigal son."

She also acutely understands the essential truth that we must yield everything to God:

> God was waiting for me to come to the end of myself and cry out to Him, "God, I can't take this anymore!" It's as though God said to me, "Good, I never said you could. I always said I would do it through you, but you must first give it to Me." In that place of yielding surrender, I gave my adult child over to God. What happened next was one of His greatest gifts. Peace in the midst of pain. It's the reality of the Christian life.

Judy ended her e-mail to me, saying,

> Allison, the greatest gift you can give your son is to pray for him and let God work. As painful as this has been for us, I wouldn't trade a moment for what God has done in our lives and how He has used this awful pain to minister to thousands of women across the USA. I have a great support system of parents who have gone through or are going through the same things. Be encouraged. This is indeed an epidemic in our country...but we cannot put a timetable on God's sufficiency.

Although we cannot put a timetable on God's grace and sufficiency for our lives, we can put a timetable on the specific changes needed to restore our home lives to peace. We can, and should, place a timetable on transitioning the current cyclone of circumstances into a calm breeze of boundaries.

That's where an action plan comes in.

With her permission, I would like to conclude this chapter with Judy's top-ten list of things she learned as a result of her enabling journey.

WHAT I LEARNED FROM BEING A PARENT IN PAIN

1. I must remind myself every day that God is in control.

2. God has allowed my circumstances, heartbreaking as they are, to change me.

3. We are not alone. God is well aware what it's like having prodigals. Look at Adam and Eve. They had it all, and God was a perfect Father. So much for all the theories.

4. The prodigal son had no reason to leave home and rebel. His dad loved him, he had a wonderful home life, plenty of money, and purpose for living. He rebelled because there is pleasure in sin for a season. The father never chased after his son or filled his pockets with money or financed his sin. He stayed put and gave his son to God.

5. God is the only One who can change our kids. Out of the kindness of His will, He alone brings us to repentance. We must pray for God to bring our adult children to the end of themselves and to deal with their problems.

6. The Enemy is at work, but he is not more powerful than God. Satan must ask God's permission to test us (see the book of Job).

7. I can't put a timetable on my prayers. Some may be answered on the other side of eternity. God is faithful, and we must pray with great faith. He is working.

8. God has changed me greatly. The heartache of living with a prodigal threw me into God's Word—big time. In the last 15 years I have devoured God's Word on a daily basis and developed a prayer life. All this to say, this experience has been a good thing for me spiritually. Whereas I once spent that time in anxiety and depression, I have now taken that time to become anchored in God.

9. God has supernaturally changed me through His Word and changed my perspective on the whole trial.

10. Yielding everything to God is the only way to peace. The day we came to our wit's end and gave our son 100 percent to the Lord was the day a miracle occurred. We were flooded with His peace, the kind that cannot be explained. We knew then why Jesus came: not only to save our souls but to give us His power to live through anything. Since that time, we have had to do that again and surrender our grandchildren. His grace is sufficient for all things. He is all we need.

12

Developing an Action Plan

There we have it, the Six Steps to SANITY:

S = STOP your own negative behavior (especially the flow of money!)

A = ASSEMBLE a support group

N – NIP excuses in the bud

I = IMPLEMENT rules and boundaries

T = TRUST your instincts

Y = YIELD everything to God ("let go, and let God")

Now it's time to develop the plan that will enable us to implement these crucial steps.

As we do, the key is to remain cool, calm, collected, and in control during this vital stage. We cannot jump in and declare to our adult children, "Enough is enough! That's it! I'm not going to take this anymore. Your days here are numbered, mark my words!"

By the time we reach this stage, many of us may feel like saying words to that effect, but the truth is that our adult children have been "marking our words" for years. They've experienced more than one of our periodic meltdowns, when their actions have backed us (yet again) against the wall, leading us to lash out in anger, fear, and frustration.

But because we love our adult children so much, it doesn't take long for us to calm down and see the error of our ways in lashing out. Soon we may even have found ourselves apologizing for our outbursts. And typically our adult children have heard this type of apology a time or two before, and they are poised and ready to respond appropriately. Some use the manipulative tool of remorse, aiming to get our sympathy.

"Yeah, I'm sorry too, Mom [or Dad]. It's just that…," and thus begins yet another discussion rife with a blend of reasons, excuses, and remorse that return things to "normal"—or at least back to where they were before our outburst.

Thus, the status quo has once again been restored.

Other adult children will quickly grab the baton of power you have unwittingly passed to them with your hasty apology—once again free to respond with their own righteous indignation at how little you understand their unique predicament, how you must not care at all about what's going to happen to them, and so on and so on.

Therefore, we must come to the table as cool, calm, and collected adults with a well-developed written plan that clearly indicates our goals. Above all, we must speak this new plan in love and not in heated anger or frustration.

A strategic action plan for a business or an organization assists a company to (1) review where it is, and (2) define where its owners want to go. It helps to give them direction, to keep them on course. It's a map, a blueprint to keep them on target, on goal, and on the ball.

Too often in homes where a dysfunctional adult child resides (or influences from afar), there is no action plan. Or if there is, it changes with the wind. It has no teeth, no credibility. In this case, the boy who cried wolf looks suspiciously like the parents.

A number of years ago, I had a job as a professional fundraising executive, and a significant part of my job was to assist board members and nonprofit organizations in the development and implementation of detailed strategic plans. I frequently conducted board retreats and planning workshops to troubleshoot and identify dysfunction within organizations, helping groups and individuals establish detailed plans to better equip their organizations to succeed. Today my strategic planning workshops are still said to be some of the best available in equipping writers, speakers, and small-business owners to succeed.

Over the years I tried to implement some of these techniques to "help" my son. I would frequently help him develop life plans and to-do lists to get his life on track—even going so far as making lists for him myself. As if that was ever going to help him! I now see that my need to keep him on track was just that—*my* need. He had no ownership of the plan, no ownership of the to-do lists. During the times I encouraged him to develop his own to-do lists (more like forced him under duress of grounding or some other punitive punishment), the consequences were either nonexistent, too severe, or had no teeth.

I was unable to see how my desire to help him succeed was actually crippling him. Moreover, for a long time I was unable to see clearly how my own personal issues were contributing to the turmoil in our household. I needed direction, healing, and hope, but instead for years I filled the empty places in my heart and soul with everything but those things. It was far less painful to focus on my son and what he needed to do with his life than it was for me to point the spotlight on my own life.

Today, with the retrospective wisdom that comes from having walked the rough terrain of enabling, I can see a better way to synthesize planning into our lives as enabling parents who desire to stop the insanity and get off the gerbil wheel of fruitless activities.

So, let's get started.

Let's quickly review three primary areas in changing our enabling behavior. Remember, we're talking about changing our own behavior, not that of our adult child.

How We Can Stop

1. Make a commitment to change.

2. Hand it over to God.

3. Get help for ourselves.

4. Follow the Six Steps to SANITY.

5. Focus on love.

What We Need to Know

1. It won't be easy.

2. We are not alone.

3. There will be consequences, and some may be painful.

4. We have rights.

5. God is in control.

What We Need to Do

1. Attend support-group meetings.

2. Read, research, and acquire knowledge.

3. Develop a written action plan.

4. Be consistent.

5. Speak the truth in love.

Remember this: You are bringing your plan to the *judgment* table and not to the *negotiating* table. The document you and your spouse (if applicable) are going to develop isn't open for discussion or negotiation. You are the adult, and this is your home. It's your money, your livelihood, and your future, and the time has come for you to define acceptable boundaries and to commit to them.

If you are too weak to do this alone, ask for help. Get the help of an already established support group or reliable counselor, or hire a professional interventionist, someone who is willing and able to stand in the gap for you, to be an accountability partner, or to intervene as your mouthpiece if needed.

Your attitude is key. It will help if you can

1. realize that you can hate the situation and still love your adult child;

2. have confidence that God will make a way where there seems to be no way; and

3. accept the truth that the time has come for drastic measures.

The Importance of a Written Plan

Developing an action plan isn't an idea unique to me. It's a *necessity* long recognized by professional counselors who deal with people in pain everyday.

One psychologist who deals with this issue often is Beth McHugh, who says,

> I strongly advise parents to sit down and plan a strategy. After all, the enabling has been occurring for many years, and taking the time to look at the situation objectively can only be a positive move, rather than rushing in trying to change everything at once and causing yourself more stress.
>
> First, parents should be quite clear on how they have enabled their adult children in the past and what behaviors they are still doing to keep the status quo. Once they can accept that some of the problem lies with them—the parents, and not the adult children—it becomes easier to deal with. While parents keep blaming their children, there can be little forward movement.
>
> Next, write a list of activities that you will no longer perform for your adult child. Also write a list of things you expect your adult child to perform. Then you, the parent, should calmly (!) approach your adult child and inform him that the house rules and boundaries will be changing. Remember, you as the parent can only change yourself. You cannot *make* your adult child take out the trash, but you can stop footing his cell-phone account, for example.
>
> The reason for taking your time in planning this change to the family dynamic is because it is going to be painful. You as the parent need to be as clear as possible as to what your

goals are and how to keep on track. Professional help from a psychologist in some cases may also be useful to assist you in passing through this transition period. In many cases, what you may experience as you attempt to change the ground rules is akin to a two-year-old's temper tantrum being manifested in an adult child's body. And sometimes that body may be physically bigger than yours. Planning is the key to success.

Developing an action plan was something virtually every respondent to my questionnaire strongly advised. Following are a few of their thoughts.

Pastor Bill Oudemolen has had frequent experience with this troubling issue:

> Speaking the truth in love is vital. Certainly, this is easier said than done in some cases. I would advise a parent, who truly wants to change his or her enabling behavior, to write out the issues, and perhaps even go so far as to write a script of the conversation before it occurs in order to prevent chickening out or getting overly emotional in the discussion. Another tip is finding the right time to have the discussion. Just springing it on the adult child without time to prepare for it may result in disastrous consequences. I regularly advise people to find the right time for tough communications by asking the other person to identify a "good time to talk" and giving that person the time parameters beyond which you are not willing to go. Something like this: "Say, Rebecca, your mom and I want to talk to you about something before the end of the month. What's a good time for us to talk?"

Another pastor who weighed in on this topic was Dawn Scott Jones, executive pastoral minister of Grand Rapids First Assembly of God in Wyoming, Michigan:

> First of all, coming to the realization that it's time to stop enabling an adult child is a positive step. I'm sure the parents have arrived there after a painful and sobering recognition

that the "help" being offered is not contributing to the overall well-being or improvement of life of their adult children. In the days ahead, however, this realization may become blurry again as their heartstrings are pulled, and the focus to stop enabling may become lost if they get caught up in guilt or manipulation from the adult child. So, as they start the process of change, I would suggest the following:

1. Be aware of how you as a parent are indeed enabling. Enabling parents have a dysfunction of their own to break. Make sure you recognize your own patterns.

2. Write down what behaviors you have that need to stop or change. What are the boundaries that need to be implemented? If you put it in writing, you are much more likely to follow through with your plan. Example: I will no longer lend you money.

3. Be prepared. You will be tested on every point of the changes you are making. Be ready with your answers before you ever get in the situation, and stick to them. Be ready and prepared to walk out the new changes regardless of how you are treated as a result. Predetermining your responses can help you not to waver.

4. Be strong. Understand there will be painful consequences for your adult child. It will be difficult and maybe even excruciating to see the kid you love hurting. But this is part of the process. He has to learn to stand, to become desperate enough to make changes.

5. Be supported. Tell someone what you are doing and ask the person to keep you accountable. Use him or her as a sounding board; draw on the person for support. You can't make these changes alone.

Heather Gemmen Wilson is a wife and mother as well as a noted author and speaker. She writes,

Parents need to make an action plan for independence. We need to tell our kids, "I want to help you succeed on your own." Some of those actions would be to create a budget, set a move-out date, create a to-do list (e.g., find an apartment, get help to move, submit change-of-address card to the post office, etc.) with due dates for each action. And then stick to those due dates. Name the consequences ahead of time for missing due dates (e.g., increased room and board, no use of perks at home like laundry, TV, or car, etc.).

John and Kendra Smiley travel the country as authors and speakers. Their ministry, based in Illinois, is appropriately called Be the Parent. They too are firm believers in developing an action plan:

> We must inform the adult child that the enabling behavior (whatever it might be) is coming to an end. We must give him a time line for the paradigm shift and then follow through with the change in our behavior and the consequences that will follow if the new requirements for adulthood are not met. However, we first recommend that we talk with our adult children in a loving manner—expressing love. Clearly the truth in love is key.

In *The Mom I Want to Be,* T. Suzanne Eller shared a great deal about setting boundaries. Not as punitive measures but as guidelines intended to strengthen the relationship with our adult children and make them healthy. In response to my questionnaire, she wrote,

> A parent must set boundaries. We need to begin with (1) mutual respect and (2) honesty. I won't lie about your addiction or cover it up. I will allow you to take responsibility for your actions each and every time. I won't rescue you, though I will continue to believe in and love you. These are only two boundaries. There are several more, but the intention is to expect and give what it takes to help the relationship move from unhealthy or destructive to a stronger, healthier relationship. This won't be easy, and there are steps to setting boundaries. First, we must give warning. Don't surprise adult children with new boundaries. Second, come up with

reasonable consequences and stick with them. Third, be consistent. If your consequence is that you will alert the police if they take the car and drive drunk, then you have to follow through every time. You have to call the police. No excuses. Fourth, you must have an alternative plan. If your boundary is that you will not engage in fighting and hopeless arguments, then you need an alternative to that. Consistency, consistency, consistency. Do it every time so they know you mean what you say and what to expect.

Leslie Vernick wrote,

> I encourage the parents I work with that whenever they begin to try to change the way they have related to their adult child, it is always helpful to give the child advance notice on what you are going to do differently and why. I encourage them to present these changes with an attitude of love and humility expressing concern for their child's long-term well-being. For example, a parent might say something like this: "Your mother and I love you very much. We see you struggling with some things and aren't sure how to help you. We realize that we don't always know what's best for you or how to help you get on your feet, but we do know that what we have been doing isn't working. We still aren't sure what the best thing is for you to do, but we know that right now we've been taking more responsibility for your own life than you have, and ultimately this is not good for you even if it helps you out in the short run. Therefore, we want you to know that from now on...or in two weeks...or no longer...etc."
>
> I encourage the parents to express this in the most neutral voice they can muster—not to get overly emotional or to get sucked into a discussion about these changes. I also encourage them to rehearse saying it aloud several times before saying it to their adult child. They need to be firm yet loving, without sounding angry or weak willed in their new resolve.

I've shared this feedback from others in hopes that you will be empowered to move forward with this crucial step in setting boundaries and regaining hope and healing in your home and heart. If you've reached the place where you *know* this has to happen, then the hard work has been accomplished. Many parents never reach this stage and instead continue on for years and years through crisis after crisis, and they never do come to the place where you are now—the place of commitment to establishing a plan of action.

Developing Your Action Plan

Step 1: Begin with prayer.

Step 2: Establish a firm time line to develop the action plan you are going to eventually present to your adult child. Give yourself time to communicate with your spouse and/or support group as you develop your notes. Do not rush this task, but don't drag it out either. Give yourself a deadline. For example: I will complete my action plan by [date].

Step 3: Get a stack of six legal pads, or six spiral steno pads, or a three-ring binder with six tabbed dividers—whatever system works best for you. The goal is to have six easily accessible notebooks or sections in which to separate your notes into six categories as you write. You'll want to be able to refer to your to-do list often and easily add or check off items as you accomplish them. You'll also want to add items to the plan as you think of them. Having to search through one notebook for all of this information can be time consuming and confusing.

Step 4: Identify your six legal pads, notebooks, or index tabs with these separate labels:

#1. *To do*—an itemized list of things *you* need to accomplish. This is *your* list and *not* a list you are preparing for your adult child. No matter how much you want to help, *do not begin to develop a list of things for your adult child to do.* That is his responsibility if he so chooses.

#2. *To stop*—a detailed list of *your* behaviors, habits, and issues you want to change or stop.

#3. The plan—an overview of what you will eventually present to your adult child in a contract format. Include the six areas mentioned in the fourth SANITY step as well as the six components listed later in this chapter.

#4. The consequences—a list of "What happens if…"

#5. Scripts—samples of what you'd like to say and how you plan to say it.

#6. Resources and miscellaneous—information about support-group resources, perhaps contact names and numbers and group locations, phone numbers, Web-site URLs, and other resources, such as books to read or purchase.

Step 5: Sit down with all six notebooks and start writing. If you are married, do this as a couple, perhaps taking turns writing. You might start by developing your overall to-do list, writing down things like "find a counselor," "attend a support group," "read such-and-such book," "buy new locks for the doors," "call the auto-insurance agent." Or you might wish to begin by writing down the things you want to stop, such as paying for your adult child's cell phone, doing his laundry; or feeling miserable, inadequate, or guilty.

As you begin developing your plan of action, make sure you have also successfully completed all or most of the following:

- conducted a thorough self-examination to determine your part in the enabling dynamic

- consulted with a professional regarding personal issues

- connected with a support group

- agreed on the action plan with your spouse

- written detailed notes on six tablets or legal pads (see the following steps)

- obtained emotional distance from the situation in order to make an objective assessment

- conducted role playing for presenting your action plan

- carefully reviewed all Six Steps to SANITY

- prayed, prayed, and prayed some more

Perhaps you might start writing things on the plan, such as (1) move out date, (2) begin to pay rent, and so forth. There is no right or wrong way to do this step, only that you pull out all the stops and write down each and every item that concerns you.

Step 6: Once you've finished your scripts, practice reading them aloud.

Step 7: Using your notes, type your action plan, including the consequences, in as much detail as you feel is necessary. Edit often, if necessary. You do want this to be as clear as possible. You may have a few false starts, but keep at it, revising as you go. Make this plan look like a formal contract. Make it clear to your adult child that a great deal of time, thought, and prayer have gone into the development of the plan. Do not hand him a one-page handwritten note. Think of this as a binding contract.

As you pray, talk with your spouse or counselor, and write, don't make developing this action plan so elaborate that you never get it accomplished. Set a timeframe for yourself to get the plan developed and *do it.*

Action Plan Template

Now, using the notes from your six tablets, combined with the various components below, it's time to develop your detailed action plan. This exercise will be incredibly empowering.

If you can't do it yourself, it's a good idea to get someone to type this into a clean and concise format on a computer. Make sure to include signature lines for you and your adult child to sign. If you don't have a computer, a member of your support group might be able to help you.

The Components of an Action Plan

1. Statement of purpose
2. Changes being implemented
3. What you will do

4. What you will not do

5. Resources available

6. Transition care package

1. Statement of Purpose

Begin with your apology—what you have done wrong and what you are now going to do to make it right. Speak this truth in love, not in anger. State your wish for your child's future, but specify that you've come to realize that ultimately what he chooses as his future will be up to him.

Be clear about the changes you are making. Remember, this is not the time to point fingers—remove the word *you* from the discussion as much as possible. Make this succinct—there is no need to elaborate. This is not a discussion open for debate or negotiation.

This is the time to say what you feel in love—to leave behind the anger, pain, accusations, and blame—all the negative things that have colored your world for so long.

You've crossed over. You've made that U-turn. There's no looking back.

When the time comes to present your plan, you may wish to have support-group members or a professional interventionist take part in the presentation. There is nothing weak whatsoever about asking for help from people who understand—and who care about you and your adult child.

2. Changes Being Implemented

If your adult child needs to move, tell him so and give him a firm move-out date, as well as a firm consequence if he does not. Define consequences for every item on your list. Clearly define issues such as

- what he is free to take from your home in the way of furniture and/or supplies
- storage of any items remaining

- debts/loans/tuition
- vehicle and/or insurance issues
- credit cards
- cell phone
- computer/technical items

If your adult child is permitted to remain in your home, establish new boundaries along with specific consequences for such topics as

- rent amount and due date
- food, supplies, and cooking
- house/room cleaning
- laundry
- work/school
- debt/bills
- expenses such as utilities, phone, household supplies, etc.
- overnight guests
- curfew
- mail
- time to get up in the morning
- zero tolerance for alcohol, drugs, or pornography
- exit strategy and date to move out

3. What You *Will* Do

- Pray for your adult child and love him.
- Remain consistent in your plan.
- Follow-up on all consequences as listed.
- Help him by providing...(Clearly define what you are willing to give him. See list in part 6 of the plan.)

4. What You Will *Not* Do

- Give your adult child money.

- Argue, debate, and/or negotiate whatsoever.
- Find him a place to live.
- Help him pack.
- Set up his new apartment or home.
- Cosign a lease or mortgage.
- Make excuses for him.
- Accept blame for his actions or inactions.
- Remind him of the timeframe.
- Allow him to return to your home at any time if things don't work out.

5. Resources Available

Develop a short list of resources to give your adult child. Encourage him to conduct further research into additional resources. Remember, you *are not* going to call any of these locations on his behalf or conduct online searches for him. What he chooses to do with this short list is his business. This list could include such things as

- a reading list of helpful books
- rehabilitation programs
- Web-site URLs
- psychological and/or spiritual counselors
- debt counselors
- support-group information
- prepay credit-card information

6. Transition Care Package

Be careful about this section. As enablers we will want to supply our kids with far too much. However, there are some instances when it's going to be acceptable to offer additional help to your adult child as he leaves the nest. Especially when he has basically exhibited a desire to be a responsible adult. You may have an adult child who works hard and, with a gentle nudge, may be ready for his "launch" into the world.

The goal of this transition care package is to make his transition a little easier, but not to fully fund the move. This care package may include such things as:

- a specific dollar figure for one month's rent and security
  - a loan or gift—your choice, but be clear!
- resource books, such as a Bible, books on finance, etc.
- a list of medical providers and dentists as well as copies of your child's health records
- food coupons or grocery-store gift certificates
- a wall calendar (not a costly day planner)
- a small file box containing copies of your child's
  - legal forms (e.g., birth certificate, DMV papers, etc.)
  - medical records
  - financial documents
  - other miscellaneous forms

Presenting Your Action Plan

When the day comes to finally present your adult child with your action plan, Leslie Vernick advises that "humility is the best approach." She writes,

> When we sit down to present our new action plan, it is imperative that we don't overuse the word *you,* as in *you* need to make some changes, I need *you* to stop doing this, or I need *you* to start doing this. As the parent who will be making the behavior changes, you need to inform your adult child that *you* have had a problem, and therefore *you* are going to be changing the way *you* respond and behave. Your adult child can choose to change his behavior—or not.

Judy Hampton adds,

> Parents must first form a united front and sit down together
> to develop a contract or agreement that includes all the stip-
> ulations for living at home until the prescribed move-out
> date. When this is completed, meet with your adult child
> to present the action plan and have him sign it. A signed
> contract is helpful and necessary. There are no surprises!
> Don't back down! No doubt this is going to be a hard thing
> to do, but keep in mind the higher good that is going to
> be accomplished as your adult child finally experiences the
> consequences of his choices. Don't be at all surprised if the
> decision you are making is met with huge resistance. Take
> that as a sign that you are doing what you need to do. It's also
> a good idea to have the locks changed on your home when
> your adult child moves. If this sounds harsh, ask yourself,
> "Has what I've been doing in the past worked?"

Author and speaker Sue Buchanan shares,

> We need to write out the objective and develop an action
> plan and a timeframe. Then, we must apply tough love—give
> specific deadlines and stick to them. If it's hard to have a one-
> on-one discussion—and it often is—sit down and conduct
> this meeting as you would in a business setting. For example,
> you might say something like this: "Your mother and I are
> excited about your future. We realize that we are holding you
> back from being all that God wants you to be by giving you
> a place to live and food to eat and [fill in the others]. This
> document we have developed outlines an action plan that
> will help you become a responsible adult and a contributing
> member of society."
>
> Within this plan, include things like when your adult child
> needs to begin paying for rent and food expenses. This figure
> should not be a token remuneration but comparable to the
> outside world. Identify a specific date he needs to move, and
> let him look for his living arrangement and make comparisons

and choose a roommate if necessary. Don't do it for him—
this is part of being responsible. (Note: Do *not* use the word
but anywhere in this document: "*but* we'll be here if you
need us"; "*but* we still love you"; "*but* someday you'll thank
us." This is a business document, and business documents
do not contain "but" escape clauses.)

As you present your plan to your adult child and outline the consequences, be prepared for fit throwing, from mild to wild.

It's what happens next.

13

Considering the Consequences

By presenting your plan of action to your child, you are setting him on a difficult course. He doesn't want this sort of difficulty in his life. He doesn't like obstacles to what he wants. So, yes, he will likely resist.

But you must be strong. You should know by now in your own experience that difficulty in life isn't always a bad thing. What your child perceives as difficult, you as the parent should see as the opening up of a series of opportunities your child will have to really find some meaning in his life.

Some of the greatest advances in history have been the result of someone first going through great pain or stress. What if the apostle Paul's mother had taken her son's place on that Damascus road to make life easier for him? Or what if Queen Esther had never gone to live in the palace, and instead sent her well-meaning aunt? What if Beethoven's mother had determined that composing music was too stressful for her deaf son? What if these people had never lived out their destinies but had instead given up in defeat?

What if the trials and tribulations your adult child is presently going through are intended to teach him a valuable lesson that will change the entire course of his life—not to mention the lives of generations of people? What if, like Paul, he needs to experience the pain of prison (real or imagined) to fulfill his life purpose?

There are countless examples of people from all walks of life who have changed the course of history because of their often disastrous life experiences. If their moms and dads had continually come to their rescue, keeping them from experiencing the pain that led to discovery, imagine the outcome.

There's a great scene in *Jurassic Park* when it's dino dinner time, and a goat is chained to a platform where the vicious velociraptor can easily find the main course. Dr. Alan Grant is incredulous when he says, "She doesn't want to be fed; she wants to hunt."

Could any one line be filled with more meaning? Hopefully, implementing your plan of action will stir in your child the desire to hunt, not simply to be fed. But even if your child doesn't rise to the coming occasions for growth, you will still be free from the responsibility and the consequences of his wrong choices.

Healing often comes through pain first. Physical therapy is painful, but it's always conducted for our own good. So too are God's plans always meant for our good—even when we can't understand them.

I've found that when it comes to consequences, we must address four needs on our journey to establishing healthy boundaries with our adult children:

1. The need to overcome the often paralyzing fear of consequences
2. The need to accept that there *will be* consequences and be willing to live with them
3. The need to prepare for possible consequences—positive and negative
4. The need to focus on the consequences pertaining to our lives, not just the lives of our adult children

Something to Think About

We may be hindering our adult children from living out their God-given destinies when we shelter them from the consequences of their actions.

I recently attended a writers conference in Colorado Springs and had the pleasure of sitting next to a gentleman at lunch one day who shared this thought-provoking story:

> I was visiting a friend who has a beautiful home on several acres of land. We were sitting on a bench by his pond when I commented on the geese that majestically floated nearby and sat sunning themselves on the grassy knoll.
>
> "How do you get them to stay?" I asked. "It looks like they have lots of options where they can hang out—what makes this area so special?"
>
> "Ah, that's easy." My friend frowned. "We overfeed them— stuff them until they can't fly or don't want to fly."
>
> "Well, that makes sense. I guess they've got it pretty good here."
>
> "Not really. I feel bad. Every one of these geese has missed their destiny because of me."

Now some would argue that the destiny of a goose in the big scheme of things is unimportant, but the lesson wasn't lost on me.

Many of us have been overfeeding our adult children for years, stuffing them with "things" until they can't fly away from the nest. In some instances we've made them literally fat, providing food in copious amounts, and in other instances we've made them figuratively fat by accepting continued incompetence and excuses for irresponsibility.

By protecting our adult children from the consequences of their actions, we are keeping them from experiencing their God-given destinies. And yet the mere thought of the negative consequences our adult children might experience sends many of us into a state of abject terror.

Sometimes we're overwhelmed by our negative thoughts regarding possible consequences our adult children might face. We think,

1. If I send my adult child away, he may die (from drugs, violence, and criminal behavior).

2. Without my financial help, there's no telling what my adult child will do to get money.

3. The thought of my adult child living on the street, selling her body, or landing in jail breaks my heart. I can't let that happen.

4. My own parents would end up helping him instead, and they would disown me.

The sad thing is, any of those scenarios are indeed possible. There are many negative consequences that may occur as a result of the changes you are about to make in your life that will affect your adult children. That's why it's vital to develop the list of potential consequences in your action plan as fully as possible. Review every scenario imaginable to prepare yourself. This doesn't mean you can stop the scenarios from happening; it means you can prepare yourself for the possibility they will happen.

However, please don't focus only on the potential negative consequences. Why not consider the likelihood of positive consequences? Let's not forget God's many promises to help us in times of trouble:

> Though I walk in the midst of trouble,
>   you preserve my life;
>   you stretch out your hand against the anger of my foes,
>   with your right hand you save me. (Psalm 138:7)

> I have told you these things, so that in me you may have peace. In this world you will have trouble. But take heart! I have overcome the world. (John 16:33)

Could it be that for some of our adult children, this new journey toward independence might be phenomenally freeing? Perhaps the consequences won't be as bad as we think?

La Shawn Barber has a keen insight on the world as one of our country's foremost political bloggers writing from a Christian worldview. She's young and doesn't yet have children of her own, but her wisdom is apparent in this simple statement:

If you've tried to get your adult child help and nothing has worked, then I advise you to pray, pull the net of support out from under him, and pray some more. You'd be surprised how resilient human beings can be, even *your* child. Realizing that he must sink or swim, his survival skills just might kick in—making him a world class swimmer!

We can prepare for all the likely consequences of implementing our action plans—both negative and positive—but we can never know what will happen until we take the steps needed to gain SANITY in our lives.

Leslie Vernick, in her response to my questionnaire, writes,

> When it comes to what can happen when we accept consequences, my favorite story is that of Helen Keller and her teacher Annie Sullivan. Helen's parents pampered blind, deaf Helen because they pitied her. She was undisciplined and untaught in even basic manners. In fact, she ate her food with her hands from the plates of family members. When Annie came into her life, she did not allow Helen to get away with bad manners and gave her rules, boundaries, and began to teach her "words" through sign language. It was only through discipline and structure as well as tough love from Annie Sullivan that Helen reached her fullest potential to graduate cum laude from Radcliffe College in 1904.

Leslie also shares this story and others like it in her book *How to Find Selfless Joy in a Me-First World*. She brings to mind a powerful truth that although it may have been easier in the short run for Helen's parents and family members to let her have her way for years, it certainly wasn't the best thing for her. It no doubt caused her parents great pain to see their beloved daughter going through the pain and anguish of learning, but Helen soon discovered a new world that would never have been opened to her had she been left alone to continue her negative behavior.

Granted, the consequences of some negative behaviors are considerably worse than others, especially consequences related to drug or alcohol use, and/or illegal activities.

In her work as the editor of *Marriage Partnership* magazine, Ginger Kolbaba has seen and heard more than a few classic examples of parental enabling. She writes,

> It is vital that we stick to the boundaries we set. I have a friend who had three sons involved in drugs. She and her husband—both strong Christians—set boundaries that said, "You will not live here and do drugs. Period." When the boys continued, they were kicked out. My friend cried; she suffered, but in the end, it ended up being the best thing. All the boys are now strong believers. I'm not suggesting you kick out a child. There are other boundaries. But the important thing is to live in integrity with who you are as a parent. Why would you allow someone to walk over your integrity—even if that someone is your child?

Author Don Otis advises that we must "maintain a zero-tolerance policy at home when it comes to drugs. Refuse to bail your children out of hardship, because self-inflicted pain is often what God uses to teach us what we need to learn. The consequences of life—the difficulties, trials, and hardships—are the best teachers."

When dealing with crisis situations that may include drugs, alcohol, and/or illegal activity, the following guidelines might be beneficial to consider ahead of time:

- Pray for courage and strength when you are breaking the enabling cycle.
- If your adult child has been arrested, do not bail him out.
- Call on your support group/person for intervention.
- Leave your checkbook and credit cards in your wallet. *Stop* paying for it, no matter what "it" may be.
- Step back from the situation for 48 hours before responding.

- Don't talk to your addicted child personally if you can help it. (He will try to play *Let's Make a Deal* with you.) Refuse to answer questions, argue, listen to reasons or excuses, and so forth.

- Place a script by the phone to read when your addicted child calls. Recite it and hang up.

- Get yourself to an Al-Anon or a CoDA support-group meeting right away.

- If there is no support group in your area, start one. It's empowering.

- Deal with your own issues (guilt, anger, shame, codependency, etc.).

- Learn all you can about the diseases of alcohol and drug addiction.

- Be strict with whatever you say to your adult child. Mean what you say; consistency is critical!

- Understand the definition of *enabling*. Don't do it!

- Look for small steps of success and hang on to them.

- Take care of yourself mentally, emotionally, physically, and spiritually. Get strong.

- Couples must be in agreement on an action plan.

- Remember the best medicine you can give an addict is tough love.

- The words of an addict have no truth; addicts are masters of the con.

- Just say *no*.

Developing Consequences in Your Action Plan

As you work on the consequences in your action plan, develop two lists of consequences, using the legal pad or notebook you started in the previous chapter.

First, develop a list of what-ifs that may or may not happen to you and/or your adult child. Include both positive and negative columns. For example, in the negative column you might write the following:

- "When I stop making my son's car payment, he may lose the car and get angry with me and never want to see me again."

- "If I call the police about what I suspect is stolen property, my son may get arrested and do significant time in jail."

- "If I insist that my daughter leave our home, I may be ostracized from friends at my church because they won't understand."

In the positive column you may list such things as the following:

- "My son may begin to feel a sense of self-respect that will transfer into the way he lives."

- "My marriage may take a turn for the better as my spouse and I focus on taking care of ourselves."

- "We may have the money to repair the garage roof now that we aren't paying added expenses to support our daughter and her husband."

The second list of consequences will be far more difficult to develop, but it is crucial to gaining SANITY in your life. You must develop a list of definitive boundary-breaking consequences you will establish in your action plan. These consequences are the non-negotiables you develop after prayer, discussion, deliberation, and 100-percent commitment. For example,

- "If you do not pay your cell-phone bill on time, we will cancel the account immediately, and you will have to establish your own cell-phone account elsewhere."

- "You will be required to pay $XX for rent, utilities, and [other] due on [date]. If this amount isn't paid on time, you will be evicted and will have XX days to move out." (See Sheriff Cook's following comment regarding eviction.)

- "If drugs are found in our home, we will call the police."
- "If we suspect stolen property is being brought into our home, we will call the police to investigate."
- "We will cease to pay your automobile insurance by [date]."

This list of consequences must be very specific and should coincide with the action plan you have developed. Remember, this is not a document up for debate or negotiation with your adult child. Once you have decided on the specifics and have typed them into a formal contract-style document, you must be prepared to stand by them no matter what.

Developing a list of consequences is vital; sticking with them is crucial.

I asked Sheriff Richard Cook about evicting an adult child, and he offered this advice:

> If drugs, other illegal activity, or physical abuse is present, call the police or the sheriff, and an order of protection will be issued. Your adult child can be kicked out of your home on the spot. However, if he refuses to be responsible and you have reached the point where you are simply tired of the same old song and dance, and you want him to move, you need to go through the formal eviction process, even if it's your home and he is your child.

We have no idea how our adult children will come out on the other side of this new journey. Many will shine like bright diamonds when the black dust of negative choices is removed. Some will experience great difficulty during the transition, and others will flourish with newfound independence and self-respect. Still others may experience great physical and emotional pain, which won't be easy for us to watch. There is also the horrific fear every parent has that an adult child won't make it—a fear realized by Steve and Lynne Johnson:

> We found out our son was using drugs and alcohol heavily at the age of fifteen. We were shocked. Our son was raised

in a wonderfully loving Christian home, where affirmation flowed daily, yet respect and discipline were taught. We could not figure out why he would choose to walk a path that was so destructive to himself and contrary to our lifestyle and beliefs. We went through every emotion during the next 12 years. It seemed he gravitated toward the dark edge, and once the drugs captured him, he was in bondage. We did our best not to enable him. There were times we would hang up the phone or walk away. There is a vicious cycle when your adult child is at the brink of death. Any discouragement could bring the biggest fear to reality, so you do your best to keep emotion and reality in balance. It got to the point, though, that when he threatened to "end it all," we had to release him to the Lord and walk away. We couldn't allow the instability of our beloved son to bring us to financial ruin—we were already emotionally and mentally bankrupt. As parents, we want so much for our kids to be "normal" by society's standards that we are trapped by our overwhelming love and dreams for them, praying that a miracle will happen, hoping that their broken hearts will someday be whole.

Steve and Lynne may never have whole hearts because a drug overdose took the life of their son at the age of 27.

Loss of life—the most painful of consequences.

Such was also the case with Marjorie. Her parents refused to give her any more money, having exhausted most of their retirement savings. When faced with financial ruin as a result of her gambling addiction, this divorced mother of two drove her car to an abandoned garage, attached one end of a garden hose to the exhaust pipe of her car, and stuck the other end through a crack in the window. Her lifeless body was discovered one week later.

The fear we feel as parents in pain is real.

Every time the phone rings late at night or there is a knock on the door when no one is expected, I fear this is the time I will have to identify my son's body at the morgue. I've relived this horrifying dream so many times that my heart is numb.

The world is at best an amazing place filled with opportunity and wonder, and at worst a fearful place teeming with evil and despair. The consequences of poor choices can range from the loss of a job to a loss of life, and God help us as parents when we take on the responsibility for the negative choices our adult children make.

God help us.

Because it's not our fault if our adult child didn't wake up in time to get to his job and he gets fired and therefore doesn't get paid and therefore can't pay his child support and therefore gets arrested. It's not our fault if he doesn't have clean clothes to wear to his job interview or enough gas in his car to get to work. It's not our fault if his cell phone gets shut off for nonpayment or he gets evicted for not paying his rent. It's not our fault if he fails another class because he didn't stay home to do his homework and instead went out to party. It's not our fault if he says yes to the drug pusher who hands him a dirty needle or if he gets behind the wheel of an automobile while drunk and ends up killing an innocent bystander. It's not our fault if he gets caught up in illegal activity that lands him behind bars, and it's not our fault if he sees suicide as his only way out of the bondage that is holding him prisoner.

The list of "It's not our fault if…" could go on for pages. However, if we continue to slide into our adult children's lives as ever-present safety nets, shielding them from the consequences of their choices, then perhaps some of the fault does rest precariously on our shoulders.

It's time our adult children begin accepting the consequences of their actions—no matter what. We must stop being safety nets. Author Rebekah Montgomery writes in her response to my survey,

> It's hard to allow our adult children to accept responsibility for their choices because the persistent picture in a parent's head is that of getting the call to come down to the morgue and identify the body of their child. And then there is the haunting specter of our adult child in a jail or prison cell being raped or brutalized by a vicious sociopath. Yet as parents we can't torture ourselves with doubt and what-if

fantasies. God's people are people of hope because we can take our concerns to God in prayer, and when we do, we know He's right there with us wanting our child to be healed and whole. If anyone understands the broken heart of a parent, it is God the Father, who has a passel of unruly brats—one of which may be our child.

"I know a woman whose two unmarried daughters are currently pregnant. One girl is in high school and the other in college," Heather Gemmen Wilson shared.

> Both girls are going to live at home and let their mother take care of the kids while they continue school. The boyfriends are welcome to visit as often as they like "without any pressure to marry the girls." The girls' mother is very disappointed that she has to quit her job to stay home with the babies, but she doesn't want her daughters to resent their choice for life, so she feels it's important to help them as much as she can. "I'm taking them to Florida over spring break because I want their lives to feel as normal as possible," she told me.
>
> These girls and their boyfriends have been let off the hook. Zero consequences. They are feeling no responsibility whatsoever for their actions. I share the mother's desire to support the kids and to make them glad they chose life over abortion, but I would do it another way. I would let the girls and their boyfriends behave as adults. They are excited to be parents, and I would encourage that without taking away the responsibilities that come with parenthood.

Author and speaker Donna Partow shared a story about her enabling mother:

> My parents, who grew up in the Depression, never wanted their kids to suffer any pain. Therefore, they constantly rescued us from the painful consequences of our behavior. My mother tells a story that is both hilarious and revealing. One of my brothers was suspended from high school for smoking

pot. He swore to the high heavens that he had not been smoking pot. So at his word, my mother went marching into the principal's office to demand the suspension of my brother's suspension. The principal looked at my mother, then at my brother, and said, "But I saw you with my own eyes with a joint [marijuana cigarette] in your hand!" To which my brother responded, straight-faced, "Yeah, but I wasn't smoking it. I was just passing it."

If the principal had caught him joint-in-hand, why drag my mother into it? Because we had learned that, if they possibly could, our parents would find a way of escape for us. Not because they didn't love us but because they did. There were eight of us kids, and some of us were crippled by that love; others decided to parent differently.

Deciding to parent differently—a key ingredient in making the changes needed to stop our enabling behavior.

It's never too late to parent differently.

14

Other Vital Issues

The great writer Leo Tolstoy began *Anna Karenina,* one of his most noted novels, with these immortal words: "All happy families are alike, but an unhappy family is unhappy after its own fashion."

How true of families with dysfunctional adult children. Each family will have its own variables that make its situation unique. One size does not fit all when it comes to dealing with a host of sometimes complicated problems that are the harvest of a family in crisis. Your action plan may resemble another family's, but it will bear the distinct imprint of your family's needs and challenges.

In this chapter I want to briefly touch on some of the variables that may need to be addressed in your situation. Particularly, let's consider the following situations:

- when drugs and/or alcohol are involved
- when your child is disabled
- when your adult child is a college student
- when little children are involved
- when blended families come together

When Drugs and/or Alcohol Are Involved
Substance abuse is rampant among families with dysfunctional

adult children. If drugs or alcohol are part of your mix, then believe me, I do understand the challenges you face.

I'd like to suggest that if you've not already done so, become extremely well educated on substance abuse. If you still have a teen in the family—particularly if you're reading this book because you have an out-of-control teen—I would encourage you to start by reading Stephen Arterburn and Jim Burns's book *How to Talk to Your Kids About Drugs,* a powerful resource that will help educate and empower you to take back your life...and to help your teen once again find his or hers. Even if your adult child is no longer a teenager, the wisdom the authors impart is vital. When your child is addicted, you, the parents, are also inescapably involved at some level.

Sheriff Cook reminds parents,

> The drug and alcohol component is almost universal in this dynamic and can escalate into very severe problems. Parents can become victims of their own enabling, because if the adult child is living with them and he is storing stolen property or harboring drugs, he could be harming himself. The parents would also come under suspicion. If it's serious, the parents could be looking at long-term consequences, such as forfeiture of their vehicle or loss of their home, say, if methamphetamine is being manufactured in their home. A home can be destroyed beyond repair, chemically overdosed as it were. Making excuses for addicts can be a very costly mistake for parents.

The drug and alcohol component played a large part in my own life during the years I was searching to fill the emptiness in my heart and soul—the years my son was a child and then a rebellious teen. I wasn't surprised, then, when they became issues in my son's life as well. The guilt I felt over my own choices held me in bondage, keeping me on the merry-go-round of enabling my son because I blamed myself for his lot in life. I hadn't lived a very sober life, so what right did I have to insist that he should? Very wrong thinking.

But I wasn't alone. Many in my generation—and yours—turned to substances to ease our pain, or simply because it was what one did as a young person: experiment.

But for many of us, the result of our experimenting has been a tailspin into the pit of depravity and despair, birthing a generation of lost and irresponsible children, who also chose to numb their pain with drugs, alcohol, and wasted pursuits. For many of our adult children, this is a cruel and painful world, and checking out of reality is far more attractive than dealing with the issues that cause them pain.

Many of them have never finished their "experiment" with drugs and are now addicts and alcoholics. Some are even drug dealers. Parents in pain often prefer to hide their heads in the sand when it comes to this issue. It's a rude awakening for parents when they stop the masquerade and look the drug and alcohol issue square in the face.

But I only wanted to help.

In some instances, drug and/or alcohol abuse has stunted the emotional growth of our adult children, handicapping them in a way that compels us to continually come to their rescue.

My child is sick; I can't throw him out on the street in this condition.

Drug and alcohol abuse is a huge part of the reason so many of our adult children have financial problems. It's difficult to keep a job when they're high or drunk, and they can't get high without buying drugs or booze, but they can't get the money to buy drugs or booze unless they have a job or some other source of income, such as illegal activity or ready access to the Bank of Mom and Dad.

It's a vicious cycle that must end now.

Let's not forget the criminal component. Addicts will steal from anyone (including us) to get the money for their next fix. Have you ever bailed your adult child out of jail because he was arrested for being in possession of someone else's drugs? (Of course they weren't his drugs. He doesn't do drugs; he was holding them for "someone else.") Besides the bail money, we have taken on the cost of hiring lawyers, paying restitution in some cases, and incurring other related expenses, such as vehicle-impound fees, required toxicology screenings, and urinalysis tests.

In the case of adult children who do admit to drug use and are backed into a corner where they must choose between prison or inpatient treatment, many parents have taken on the cost of the treatment center. Most medical-insurance companies don't cover inpatient treatment, and chances are your adult child is no longer being covered on your medical-insurance policy anyway. Parents are going into severe debt to pay for long-term treatment for their children, in some instances more than once. Many parents and grandparents have exhausted their life savings, including their well-earned retirement benefits, to pay for unsuccessful rehabilitation programs for adult children who have no desire to change.

Many questionnaire respondents shared horror stories about family and friends losing their homes after mortgaging everything to pay for yet another unsuccessful long-term rehabilitation program or paying the costly legal fees to keep their adult child from serving time in prison as a result of his or her actions.

Yes, many of our adult children are hurting—they are in pain, and they need help. However, we must stop feeling responsible for the continued self-destructive choices they are making.

They can get help if they want it.

Lest you think I'm a coldhearted individual who needs a house dropped on her, I'm behind any parents who want to help their adult children get treatment for an addiction but not enable them. It is enabling plain and simple, however, when we continue to dole out the cash, in some instances significant amounts of cash, each time they need help.

Since 1998, the REACH Foundation (Recovery, Education, Action, Career, and Help) has had a mission to help substance-addicted persons who are committed to recovery get their lives back on track by providing funds for treatment and education. The target beneficiaries are addicts and alcoholics who are economically challenged. The REACH Foundation provides financial assistance for treatment and scholarships for education. Their end goal is to help individuals stay sober and productive for the rest of their lives.

I met with Carl Mosen, the founder of REACH, and Stacy Brower, the REACH board chairperson. Carl recently celebrated 25 years of sobriety, and Stacy is an ex-enabler whose adult child, now clean and sober, is serving as a professional drug-and-alcohol-abuse counselor.

Stacy told me,

> When it comes to dealing with adult children who have drug and/or alcohol abuse issues, I think the main contributing factor we must get over is fear. We fear our children won't love us if we don't help them. We fear they'll get into serious trouble, go to jail, or even die if we don't help. Another contributing factor is our lack of understanding when it comes to addiction. We're uninformed about the pathology of addiction. Most parents are at a loss as to what we can do to help our child. We want to believe we are dealing with children we know and love, yet the reality is that addiction distorts how the addict thinks and feels. The person we are dealing with is not the person we raised.

Years before developing REACH, Carl Mosen founded Sober Living by the Sea, an organization dedicated to treating and rehabilitating alcoholics. Mosen says, "[Alcoholism] has been a crippling plague sweeping our nation for decades, but the component of parents and grandparents taking on the majority of the responsibility is relatively new—yet growing in phenomenal numbers."

We should never give up hope that our adult children will find a way out of the dark abyss of addiction. We should never stop encouraging them, emotionally supporting them, and loving them. And we should never stop praying for them. Miracles happen every day, and God will make a way where there seems to be no way.

However, there is a difference between remaining hopeful and emotionally supportive and bearing the acute financial responsibility of drug or alcohol rehab time and time again.

The bottom line for parents of an addicted adult child is that you will need to become very educated regarding your child's addiction and consider how his or her addiction will affect the boundaries you set and the action plan you write.

When Your Child Is Disabled

Another vital issue for some parents is that their adult child is either emotionally or physically disabled. In such cases, the distinction between enabling and helping may be blurred. In writing your action

When it comes to the drug and alcohol component, there are numerous books to help you learn more about how to deal specifically with this issue. Yet here are a few questions to consider if you're not sure how involved your adult child is with drugs:

Does your adult child...

- drive a nicer car and work fewer hours than you do?
- have all the latest expensive technology toys, yet earns barely more than minimum wage?
- have strangers looking for him at all hours of the day and night?
- have an odd look about him, in his eyes, skin tone, and mannerisms?
- sleep a lot, yet exert very little energy to be that tired?
- fly off the handle and behave erratically?
- have more excuses than Imelda Marcos has shoes?

If you've answered yes to several of these questions, you need to confirm that your adult child is involved in substance abuse and add it to the mix of your action plan. If your child is living at home, the most certain boundary you set will be the removal of any habit-forming substances from your home and an insistence that while your adult child lives under your roof, use of such substances will not be tolerated.

plan, you need to be clear about what your disabled adult child can and cannot do for himself, particularly as it relates to the future.

Can he eventually assume more responsibility, even full responsibility for himself? The extent to which he can do so needs to be spelled out in your plan, and boundaries must be set with that goal in mind. What do your disabled child's doctors say? Can he be trained to be entirely self-sufficient? Start now working toward that goal by setting the necessary boundaries for him and the limits to which you will help (not enable) him to reach the level of independence he can reasonably attain.

Be knowledgeable about the resources and support groups that pertain to your child's disability. Is he bipolar? If so, to what extent? Can he become independent by using prescribed medication? Is there a local group to which he can become accountable and find support for his disability?

Make sure you have a proper diagnosis of your child's disability. Consult more than one doctor. Ask questions. Explain to your child's specialist that you are writing a plan to move your child to as much independence as his disability will allow, and you need the specialist's specific advice. Be clear on the prognosis for your child. Is this disability permanent, or can it be reversed?

Find out from other parents of children with this disability what has worked for them. Remember, though, that you're doing this not as further enablement but to simply determine exactly what boundaries you can reasonably expect your disabled adult child to understand.

Remember too that in some cases "disabled" may simply be a catchall term with little real meaning. Do not allow your child to make the diagnosis that he is disabled. Many who are labeled "disabled" may in fact be totally capable of the full range of "abled" responsibilities.

When Your Adult Child Is a College Student

In horror, my husband and I watched a recent *20/20* TV special on the rise of alcohol and drug addiction among college students. The exposé showed party after party in pubs, frat houses, dorm rooms, and other locations and cited cold, hard facts from studies conducted by reputable organizations. Clearly, the issue is reaching epidemic proportions on campuses across the country.

Understanding what alcohol intoxication does to a mind and body, I couldn't imagine it would be easy for many of these young people to get up for classes the morning after a party or to be responsible when it came to studying and taking tests. From the many interviews conducted with parents around the United States, it was evident that many of these party students are failing school in record numbers.

To that I say, "The buck stops here"...with my pocketbook.

If you are funding your adult child's education and/or his housing on or off campus, a clear boundary must be established in which a specific grade-point average must be maintained or no further financial assistance will be given.

It's a privilege—not a mandatory entitlement—for our adult children to go to school and have parents subsidize all or part of the expenses. It's time our adult children belly up to a different kind of bar and either reach the expectations you set for them or take the entire financial responsibility themselves.

Leslie Vernick shared how her wise father handled her college expenses:

> I was the oldest, and for college my father told me I would have to contribute to my education costs. He said he'd pay three-quarters of the first year, half of the second year, a quarter of the third year, and my final year I was on my own. Knowing the ground rules ahead of time helped me prepare with scholarships, savings, and loans and also made me take responsibility for my education sooner than had he paid the entire bill. I also knew that college wasn't just a party or a free ride and that if I didn't really want to be there, I shouldn't go, because I would have to pay for much of it myself.

A professor changed the life of noted blogger La Shawn Barber who shared the following in her response to my survey:

I vividly recall sitting in class one day when a college English professor let our entire class have it. He said we were "lazy and undisciplined." He said that many of our hard-working parents were paying for us to be here, and we didn't care, coming to class with incomplete assignments and failing tests. He said we ought to be ashamed for wasting time partying and hanging out instead of taking advantage of our educational opportunities. I was ashamed, and from that day forward, I made more of an effort. I wasn't a genius, but my grades drastically improved. To this day, I remember Dr. Hutson. Without even realizing it, he taught me what being a responsible, contributing member of society really meant.

I recently listened to another news report about the growing epidemic of alcohol abuse on college campuses today, especially concerning students living in sorority or fraternity houses. The resident doctor of the news network was reporting on a recent study conducted by her alma mater, a study that reported a record increase in alcohol consumption among college students. When asked by the host of the program what parents should do, the doctor said, "Parents need to tell their children about the dangers of alcohol and..."

I tuned her out as she began rattling off platitudes, thinking, *No! That is not the answer!*

By the time our adult children are college students living on or off campus, with or without roommates, in sorority or fraternity houses or not, no amount of "telling them" is going to mean a hill of beans if they are involved in excessive partying.

However, as I said earlier, if we are subsidizing their education or campus living expenses, we can dictate what grade-point average must be maintained for us to continue funding their advanced education. Remember the golden rule: he who has the gold rules.

Another issue on college campuses around the country is the issue of "helicopter parents." If you have a tendency to hover over your kids in anxious anticipation of fulfilling an unmet need, your intentions may be honorable, but your behavior may earn you that unwanted moniker of "helicopter parent."

Helicopter parents are obsessed with their children and become overly involved in their lives. They overstep the boundaries of acceptable parental participation in their children's lives.

This conduct may have been encouraged when your child was in kindergarten, but now that he is in college, you may find yourself being treated as persona non grata if you don't back off and let him learn to live his own life.

"You must remember that college is a time for your child to become an adult. If you are constantly helping him avoid any sort of discomfort by treating him like a child, he will still be a child when he graduates. So, as much as you think you are showing love, you are actually crippling him for life," says Boyce Watkins, a professor at Syracuse University and author of *The Parental 411*.

Hovering also sounds very suspiciously like the actions of a parent who is either already enabling their adult child or establishing a pattern of enabling.

Stay Out of It

Amy Tiemann, author of *Mojo Mom,* says that parents would do equally as well to cut the electronic umbilical cord once their kids move out of the house. A daily call is okay, she says, but don't call so often that your kid is spending more time on the phone with you than experiencing the freedom of college life.

"Unless there is a genuine crisis involving serious health and well-being issues, parents should not intervene in academic or residential issues," Tiemann adds. "This means staying out of grading disputes or roommate arguments."

Some colleges are even hiring a dean of parents, whose job it is to focus on parental complaints about roommates, expenses, and their child's emotional well-being, says Stacy DeBroff, CEO of Mom Central, Inc., a national mom expert and regular guest on the *Today Show.*

"There comes a point when as parents, we just have to let go and hope we've taught our children well enough that they have problem-solving skills, without always relying on parents to intervene," DeBroff says.

"Parents need to know that hovering and interfering send the message that their adult children are incompetent to handle their own lives," Tiemann says. "Being supportive is great, but it is important to realize that this is a new phase of life that requires independence."

When Little Children Are Involved

When our adult children behave irresponsibly and they have children of their own—our grandchildren—it adds a level of concern to our lives that cannot be ignored. What do we do when young children are involved? How should we advise parents who say the following:

- "If we didn't buy groceries for our daughter, our grandchildren wouldn't have food to eat."
- "We're happy to keep our grandchildren overnight, but it breaks our hearts when they don't want to go back to their own home and cry to stay with us."
- "What rights do I have to keep my grandchildren with me when their parent comes to pick them up and is clearly under the influence of something?"

Such situations may indicate a need to bring in an outside agency such as the Department of Social Services (DSS). If you do take this step, be aware that there may be legal ramifications. In cases such as those I just described, I would still encourage you to define your ultimate goal, seek the advice of a legal professional, and work out a plan of action.

I have a grandson by my son's past girlfriend who will be starting kindergarten this fall. He lives in my town, yet the circumstances are convoluted, and I don't get to see him very often. It breaks my heart not to be an active part of his life. It breaks my heart that the father he knows, my only son, is so troubled and lost.

Often, when grandchildren are involved, there is a tug-of-war between the grandparents and parents, placing the innocent child (or children) in the middle as an unwitting victim in what can at times be a bitter and dangerous battle.

I have a dear friend who, along with her husband, is raising their granddaughter. I asked her the following questions:

Question: When you have a dysfunctional adult child who is raising your grandchild, and you realize that his behavior is causing serious emotional, psychological, and perhaps even physical danger to your grandchild, what do you advise a grandparent to do?

Answer: Make that call—to the police, social services, or other agency. Do whatever you have to do to protect an innocent child. You may not know what lies at the end of the tunnel if you make the call, but you can bet your bottom dollar that you know what's at the end of the tunnel if you *don't* make the call.

Question: What is the most difficult aspect of raising a grandchild in this situation?

Answer: We deal every day with the dynamics of emotional dysfunction with our precious granddaughter. Every day. That means we have to work twice as hard at raising her as we had to work at raising our children. There are also the legal ramifications. I would have to say we spend no less than one hour a day and sometimes up to five hours a day dealing with the various legal offices. There are the what-to-do-if-Mom-or-Dad-shows-up issues. It's now easy for Mom to think she can swoop in at any given moment and be as much of or as little of a mother as she desires. So we have to guard our granddaughter while at the same time allowing her to have *some* contact with Mom (as the court allows). If we aren't careful, she will use Mom or Dad as her "I'll just go live with…" alternative when she is older and gets angry.

Question: What advice in general would you care to share with other grandparents who are raising their grandchildren or are considering doing so?

Answer: Don't forget who *you* are and who your *spouse* is. Take some time for yourself. And enjoy it. You've made some hard choices—first to turn your child over to the authorities, if necessary, and then to actually do the parenting thing all over again. You know more now than before. You know what hills to die on. You know what moments to cherish. So cherish them!

That said, there are no easy answers to this dilemma. My advice is to stay connected with your support group and talk about the specific issues you're confronting. Meet with a trusted clergy member, and by all means talk with a legal professional about what recourse you have available, considering your circumstances. Think and pray about this very carefully, and always remember to act out of love in every situation. If a young child is in any kind of danger—emotional, psychological, or physical—do not hesitate to do what it takes to remove the child from harm's way.

We must always remember the verse in the Old Testament book of Esther, "For such a time as this...," for it could be that you have been placed in the life of this young child to be his or her advocate "for such a time as this" (4:14).

Pray without ceasing about this life-changing possibility.

When Blended Families Come Together

Blended families add yet another dimension of challenges and often indulgences. Some moms and dads feel a bit of guilt over a split in the family, and they sincerely want to make up for it by giving their kids more material things and more money.

Then we have parents with entirely different parenting skills bringing together children from previous marriages. When children with entirely different upbringings are brought together under one roof, you can almost guarantee friction.

How do parents and stepparents cope? How do the "yours, mine, and ours" kids live together in harmony?

Again, this is where some written expectations may prove helpful. If the situation with your adult child is affecting your blended family, particularly if there are other children involved, it may be necessary for family members to work out a separate plan of action for themselves, apart from the plan regarding the adult child. Obviously, if an ex-spouse is the other birth parent of the dysfunctional adult child, that adds one more potential source of difficulty. However, most problems that arise come about because of a lack of clear expectations. Again, having those expectations written down and addressed in a plan of action may solve or even prevent a whole host of problems.

Every Family Is Unique

There are no doubt many other variables and vital issues that could be part of your family's story. It would be impossible to address every conceivable situation, but God knows every detail about your family—and your adult child.

I fully believe that in every family and in every problem in every family, God has a way of bringing about healing and restoration. I think you must realize by now that in my own case, the story has not yet been completed. Our family has done what we can. We have walked through the SANITY steps outlined in this book, and besides our daily prayers for my son, that's all we can do.

But in the meantime, our lives are not just on hold. We're busy, productive, and *happy*. We've made the decision and implemented the action plan that has allowed us to move on with our lives. That's what I want for you too. I'd like to think that a year from now, most of you will be in a far better place than you are as you read this. I'm praying that your decision to take back your life from your adult child will have brought some freedom to your experience that you don't have right now.

You are in for an adventure. There will be some pain ahead, but also the freedom that comes from setting boundaries with your adult child.

Be free.

Epilogue

I'm not sure I fully comprehended the healing power of Scripture as it applies to current issues in our lives until I read Carol Kent's book *When I Lay My Isaac Down*. Because I know Carol personally, I have been able to view her life before, during, and after the profound story that is the basis of her book. I've stood in a prayer circle around her as she kneeled on the floor, unable to stand, weeping the tears of pain only a parent can know. If you have not yet read her book, please do.

Although I had read the biblical story of Abraham many times, I didn't fully appreciate the reality of what it must have meant for him to take his son Isaac up that mountain. What it must have felt like to build an altar, tie up his son, lay him on the wood, and prepare to kill—to sacrifice—his own flesh and blood with a knife.

In her book, Carol says, "That whole mental picture sends shivers of horror up my spine. It seems so bizarre and so matter-of-fact. So brutal and so insane. It isn't natural. It isn't normal. It sounds like the craziest, most far-out, nonsensical, and horrific thing a parent could do to a child."[1]

Long before Isaac was born, God had given Abraham detailed directions and a list of wonderful promises. Abraham knew that God had a plan and a purpose for his life, and he trusted Him implicitly—

to the point of sacrificing his own son if need be. When faced with the biggest test of his life, Abraham chose faith.

And God spared Abraham's son.

In Abraham's faithfulness, in his ability to lay his Isaac down, we see God blessing Abraham and Isaac far more abundantly, making this one of the most powerful love stories in the Bible.

Carol says, "As a significant biblical character, Abraham helps me identify the role of faith in reestablishing a trust-filled relationship with God. He also helps me to see God's plan to repair the damage that has been done by sin."[2]

God has been helping me for years to repair the damage done by sin. As the compiler and editor of the God Allows U-Turns series, I have been blessed to glimpse into the lives of countless others whom God is also helping as they share their true short stories of a God who not only allows U-turns, but whose grace, mercy, and love can heal even the most broken life—or heart.

There is no doubt in my mind and heart that there is a God who loves us—sometimes in spite of ourselves. I believe that God truly is in control and that He has a specific plan and purpose for each of us. We may not always know what that is—and it may change over time—but it is nonetheless true.

It is true for us and it is true for our adult children, no matter how painful the situation may be right now. No matter how long you have been fighting this uphill battle.

This book has been in development for decades—long before I ever thought of writing it.

The experience with my own son has shaped—and continues to shape—my faith the most. This painful and intricate journey of love and enabling, which so often holds power and precedence over my heart, has been my "Isaac experience."

I was 35 years old when I made my U-turn toward God. Christopher was barely 18 at the time. As I ventured into my new life, he continued on his journey to find his way. I wish I could say that in finding faith I also found the answers to being the kind of parent my son needed. Sadly, that was not true. I continued on and off for years to come to his rescue, confusing helping with enabling. I sent mixed messages time and again, unclear of my own boundaries and thus unable to define any for my son.

It took time for me to get to the root of my own pain, to be willing to do whatever was necessary to take the focus off my son and point the microscope on my own blemished life. It took time to see how my actions often contributed to my son's out-of-control behavior. I'm a stubborn, strong-willed woman, and it's been difficult for me to step back and allow God to do what He does best: be God.

Carol Kent writes, "Our 'Isaacs' are the heart sacrifices we make when we choose to relinquish control and honor God with our choices when all seems lost."[3]

Reading Carol's book started my journey to write this one. If she could do it, then so could I. If God met her right where she was—in the middle of such anguish—then surely He could walk me through the valley of reliving the years that led me to this place.

And in so doing, perhaps I could help others, too.

I have a stack of letters from my son. If my house was on fire (you know the age-old question, "What would you grab first?"), I'd take as many photo albums as possible, and this short stack of letters from Christopher.

There's a song by Mark Schultz that makes me weep no matter how many times I hear it. It's called "Letters from War." With heart-wrenching lyrics, the song describes a mother's pain as she writes to her son in the military, long after he is captured by the enemy. She treasures the letters she received from him before his capture.

My song would have another title: "Letters from Prison."

The letters I've received from my son are written mostly in pencil on prison-issue notebook paper in tiny print, so as to fit as much as humanly possible on the limited paper supply. Called "kites" in prison terminology, some letters are sent with the stamps secured upside down; others are stamped with the name of the jail or prison on the outside.

The one I hold most dear is postmarked May 14, 2003, from a federal detention center in Oregon. I recall the day I received it as though it were yesterday.

The letter felt as heavy as my heart.

My mother had died a few short weeks before, and Chris was still unaware of her passing. I had neither the money to fly to Oregon nor the heart to tell him in a letter. He was extremely close to his grandma when his own mother was sinfully searching for answers—she had been the one constant in his life as a child. I was working with the prison chaplain to coordinate a phone call to Chris so I could tell him myself.

I'd been doing yard work— my passion. It was springtime in Minnesota; everything was lush and green. Everywhere I looked, new life had sprung from the cold ground of winter.

I sat on the picnic-table bench, holding the letter to my heart as I always did, saying the same prayer I always said.

Lord, please keep him safe. Please let him find You in all of this.

> **THE WAY OF SALVATION**
>
> John 10:10
> Romans 5:8
> John 14:6
> Revelation 3:20
>
> Pray: Father, I know that I am a sinner and I ask you to forgive me. I believe Christ died for me and I want to turn from my sins. Jesus, come into my heart and be my personal savior. I promise to obey and follow you all the days of my life.
>
> Name: Chris ****
>
> Date: April 7, 2003

As I opened his 12-page letter, a small piece of paper fell to the ground. Picking it up, a glance was all it took before the tears came. In no time I was weeping like a baby. After 31 years my son had made his U-turn—two days after my mother died.

"Sit down and get ready for some heavy stuff," his letter began.

It's been years since that letter arrived, followed by others as my son has been in and out of jail, in and out of trouble. Since then, my family and I watched as Christopher was baptized at our church, declaring his U-turn to the world.

Yet his new journey of faith hasn't been easy. I've watched him keep one foot firmly planted in the sinful ways of the world and the other gently skimming the fertile soil of faith.

God's Word is clear when it teaches us that we can't live fully for the Lord when we live in both worlds. I want so much for my son to experience the true freedom that comes when we live according to God's plan and purpose for our lives.

But that will never happen if I continue to hold on to him—coming to his rescue, trying to keep him safe.

Because that's no longer my job.

My son is an adult, and he must find his own way. I can help him best by doing less.

I can love him. I can ask him to forgive me for the part I played in making him dependent on me. I can keep my heart open and my wallet closed. I can dream big dreams for him and pray big prayers.

I can continue to hope.

I can see him for who he is, not as I want him to be.

I have an adult child who is wise, witty, and fun-loving. He is a handsome and articulate man who as a child had a kind and gentle spirit at the core of a heart now hardened by painful life experiences and sinful choices. I have an adult child who would argue that he isn't being held firmly in Satan's grip, yet I know the life he is living is not what God would want for him.

But do I know that for certain? Who am I to judge?

Perhaps it's exactly the kind of life God wants for him—for right now—for such a time as this. Perhaps his trials will one day become triumphs, changing the lives of others.

In the early part of their painful journey, Gene and Carol Kent couldn't possibly have known how their only son's tragedy would one day birth Speak Up for Hope, an organization with a mission to "give hope to the hopeless, encouragement and strength to the weary, healing to marriages that have been torn apart by incarceration, and mental, spiritual, and physical stability to the children of prisoners."[4]

Yet while they have found "unshakable faith in unthinkable circumstances" (the subtitle of *When I Lay My Isaac Down*), the fact remains that through it all they have discovered the most empowering thing they can do on a daily basis: lay down their weapons of anger and unforgiveness and embrace God's relentless love. For them and for their son.

And so I continue to pray for my adult child. I pray for another U-turn in his life. A U-turn that will open his eyes and his heart in such a way that God will be able to use him fully for His glory. And I pray to stop being the self-appointed travel guide in trying to direct my son to that place I want him to go. It's not about what I want for his life.

As Henry David Thoreau wrote, we must "step to the music we hear, however measured or far away."

God knows what He's doing.

I am not God.

I am a child of God on a journey that has brought me to a place of healing more than once. And therefore, if I want to have SANITY in my life, I must live the life God has given me to live. My life and no one else's.

I can live as the daughter of a King, and not as an abused, molested, fatherless child locked in a dark closet, looking for light in all the wrong places. Not as the victim of a violent ex-husband, but as a victor in spite of a violent ex-husband.

I can experience grace, mercy, and forgiveness afresh every day as I walk alongside God, trusting that He is in control.

I can learn from my mistakes and stop repeating them.

I can place the Word of God deep in my heart, mind, and soul by fully embracing—if not always understanding—that God has a plan for each of us, and often I must get out of His way and let Him do the work He wants to do.

And so, dear fellow parents in pain in the journey of enabling, I beseech you to start living your own lives now.

In Paul's letter to the Philippians, he said, "This is my prayer: that your love may abound more and more in knowledge and depth of insight" (1:9).

These days I'm trying my best to gain knowledge and insight, and to love more. To love my son in spite of his choices. To love my husband even when he's not being very lovable. To love my friends and family and even the strangers God places in my path, no matter how difficult it might sometimes be. It's important to love in a healthy way, and ofttimes parents in pain find that hard to do.

But mostly I'm learning how to love myself. To stop feeling guilty, stop blaming, and stop the vicious cycle of enabling.

The challenges haven't stopped; the journey to gaining knowledge and insight continues. But one thing I know: God will meet us where we are—no matter how broken, no matter how bitter.

It doesn't matter where you are in your journey of enabling an adult child. What matters is that you stop the insanity right now, today—this very minute.

You can gain SANITY and in doing so begin an amazing adventure of self-discovery.

When our priority becomes the development of an intimate relationship with Jesus, the sand in the hourglass of life shifts.

It is my prayer that in gaining SANITY, you will also gain a sense of what it means to live a life filled with love, freedom, and peace. For parents in pain, peace has existed only in brief interludes between crises.

I know. I've been there all too often.

The greatest gift we can give our adult children is to stand firm in our resolve to struggle through the pain of change.

Carol Kent says,

> If you are still clutching your Isaac to your chest, running around in circles saying, "God's not going to get what I have!" make a choice. Misery or joy? Frenetic activity or relaxation? Control or release? Codependence or God-dependence? Is the alternative to laying down our Isaacs that appealing? I don't think so.

The faith that gets us through unthinkable circumstances begins with being flat-out needy and allowing God's love to wrap us up, hold us close, and dry our tears. One day we discover that our cries are being transformed into life-giving, healthy tears that are rebirthing faith, hope, and joy. And life doesn't get much better than that.[5]

I've been flat-out needy, and God embraced me. He will embrace you, too.

Today my son drove up to my house on his motorcycle. A free man—for now. Yet a man still plagued by immense trial and tribulation, as the broken pieces of his life are once again falling around him. I shook my head as he related his latest life drama, offering nothing but a loving ear to listen. He's still making choices that break my heart and make me cry. I ache for him, wanting so much to help ease his pain. Yet I know it's through pain that God does some of His best work.

So I sit back listening, not offering advice, not judging, not coming to his rescue. It's a different mom my son is seeing this day. I silently pray for strength to maintain the boundaries I have worked so hard to develop.

"I love you," I say, hugging him close as he prepares to leave.

"I love you, too, Mom," he says. "It'll be okay; it always is."

But I want so much more for him than a life that is simply "okay." I want him to know the peace that passes understanding, the joy that comes from loving the Lord with all his heart, soul, and mind.

Yet for now I must find peace in "okay."

I must stand back and let the apples fall where they will instead of desperately trying to second-guess their descent in order to catch them so they don't bruise. That rescue dance ran me ragged for far too many years.

I stand in the driveway as my son pulls out on the street, waving good-bye.

His life may not be what I would have for him, but he's alive, and free, and I can show him what it means to love as God would have us love…with open arms. I know without a doubt that God's love will wrap me up, hold me close, and dry my tears. Because I have discovered the secret of SANITY and that no matter what happens, I am never alone. God is in control.

As my friend Carol says, "It doesn't get much better than that."

Recommended Resources

We live in an age where books are available on virtually every subject. No matter our age or life experience, we should never tire of wanting to learn more about the world in which we live—to personally grow in areas that concern and interest us. Reading is our gateway to knowledge. I encourage you to approach parenting your adult child with prayer and forethought.

A Parent's Library of Learning and Growth

1. Grow your faith: Read the Bible. Choose a version that best speaks to you.

2. Grow your knowledge of how to be the best parent possible:
   - *How to Talk to Your Kids About Drugs* by Stephen Arterburn and Jim Burns (Harvest House, 2007).
   - *Raising Respectful Children in a Disrespectful World* by Jill Rigby (Howard Books, 2006).
   - *Sacred Parenting: How Raising Children Shapes Our Souls* by Gary L. Thomas (Zondervan, 2005).

3. Grow your knowledge of boundaries:
   - *Boundaries: When to Say Yes, When to Say No to Take Control of Your Life* by Henry Cloud and John Townsend (Zondervan, 1992).

4. Grow your knowledge of how to change:
   - *The Emotionally Destructive Relationship: Seeing It, Stopping It, Surviving It* by Leslie Vernick (Harvest House, 2007).

- *The Mom I Want to Be: Rising Above Your Past to Give Your Kids a Great Future* by T. Suzanne Eller (Harvest House, 2006).
- *Whisker Rubs: Developing the Masculine Identity* by Don S. Otis (Living Ink Books, 2007).

5. *Grow your knowledge of personality types:*
   - *Personality Plus: How to Understand Others by Understanding Yourself* by Florence Littauer (Revell, 1992).

6. *Grow your knowledge of marriage:*
   - *The Five Love Languages: How to Express Heartfelt Commitment to Your Mate* by Gary D. Chapman (Zondervan, 2004).

7. *Grow your knowledge of prayer:*
   - *The Power of a Praying Parent* by Stormie Omartian— or any of Stormie's books in The Power of a Praying series (Harvest House, 2007).

8. *Grow your knowledge of how God works in a life:* Read as many personal-testimony (memoir) books as possible over the course of your life. Some powerful books on making a life-changing U-turn journey toward God including the following:
   - *Blue Like Jazz: Nonreligious Thoughts on Christian Spirituality* by Donald Miller (Thomas Nelson, 2003).
   - *Born Again* by Chuck Colson (Chosen, 2004).
   - *Girl Meets God: A Memoir* by Lauren F. Winner (Random House, 2003).
   - *I Told the Mountain to Move: Learning to Pray So Things Change* by Patricia Raybon (Saltriver, 2006).
   - *Mere Christianity* by C. S. Lewis (Harper One, 2001).

- *Stormie: A Story of Healing and Forgiveness* by Stormie Omartian (Kingsway, 2001).

- *Traveling Mercies: Some Thoughts on Faith* by Anne Lamott (Anchor, 2000).

- *When I Lay My Isaac Down: Unshakable Faith in Unthinkable Circumstances* by Carol Kent (NavPress, 2004).

Notes

Chapter 1

1. Jill Rigby, *Raising Respectful Children in a Disrespectful World* (West Monroe, LA: Howard Books, 2006), 7.

Chapter 2

1. Judy Hampton, *Ready? Set? Go! How Parents of Prodigals Can Get On with Their Lives* (Tucson: Hats Off Books, 2005), 15.

2. Henry Cloud and John Townsend, *Boundaries: When to Say Yes, When to Say No to Take Control of Your Life* (Grand Rapids: Zondervan, 1992), 249-50.

3. Pauline Neff, *Tough Love: How Parents Can Deal with Drug Abuse* (Nashville: Abingdon Press, 1982), 78.

4. Betsy Hart, *It Takes a Parent: How the Culture of Pushover Parenting Is Hurting Our Kids—And What to Do About It* (New York: Putnam, 2005), 36.

5. Cloud and Townsend, *Boundaries,* 234-35.

6. Janice Chaffee, *If the Prodigal Were a Daughter* (Eugene, OR: Harvest House, 2003), 9.

Chapter 4

1. Judi Braddy, *Prodigal in the Parsonage: Encouragement for Ministry Leaders Whose Child Rejects Faith* (Kansas City, MO: Beacon Hill, 2004), 44.

2. Braddy, *Prodigal,* 65.

3. Ibid.

Chapter 5

1. Judy Hampton, *Ready? Set? Go! How Parents of Prodigals Can Get On with Their Lives* (Tucson: Hats Off Books, 2005), 94.

2. Stormie Omartian, *Seven Prayers That Will Change Your Life Forever* (Nashville: Thomas Nelson, 2006), 45-46.

3. Omartian, *Seven Prayers,* 59.

4. Ibid., 58.

5. Hampton, *Ready? Set? Go!*, 91.

6. Henry Cloud and John Townsend, *Boundaries: When to Say Yes, When to Say No to Take Control of Your Life* (Grand Rapids: Zondervan, 1992), 251-52.

Chapter 6

1. Leslie Vernick, *The Emotionally Destructive Relationship: Seeing It, Stopping It, Surviving It* (Eugene, OR: Harvest House, 2007), 119-120.

Chapter 7

1. Co-Dependents Anonymous, "The Welcome," http://www.codependents.org.

2. Co-Dependents Anonymous, "The Twelve Traditions."

Chapter 8

1. Bill O'Reilly, *Culture Warrior* (New York: Broadway, 2006), 201-2.

2. O'Reilly, *Culture Warrior,* 1.

Chapter 9

1. John Eldredge, *Epic: The Story God Is Telling* (Nashville: Thomas Nelson, 2007), 10.

2. Eldredge, *Epic,* 11.

3. Keri Wyatt Kent, *Listen: Finding God in the Story of Your Life* (San Francisco: Jossey-Bass, 2006), 65.

4. Henry Cloud and John Townsend, *Boundaries: When to Say Yes, When to Say No to Take Control of Your Life* (Grand Rapids: Zondervan, 1992), 30.

5. Kent, *Listen,* 108.

6. Ibid., 109.

7. Cecil Murphey, *When Someone You Love Abuses Drugs or Alcohol: Daily Encouragement* (Kansas City, MO: Beacon Hill, 2004), 11.

Chapter 10

1. *The Bible Promise Book* (Uhrichsville, OH: Barbour, 1990), 158-59.

Chapter 11

1. T. Suzanne Eller, *The Mom I Want to Be: Rising Above Your Past to Give Your Kids a Great Future* (Eugene, OR: Harvest House, 2006), 91.

2. Eller, *Mom*, 36.

3. Leslie Vernick, *The Emotionally Destructive Relationship: Seeing It, Stopping It, Surviving It* (Eugene, OR: Harvest House, 2007), 192.

4. Vernick, *Emotionally Destructive Relationship*, 193.

Epilogue

1. Carol Kent, *When I Lay My Isaac Down: Unshakable Faith in Unthinkable Circumstances* (Colorado Springs: NavPress, 2004), 37.

2. Kent, *When I Lay*, 39.

3. Ibid., 12.

4. Ibid., 198.

5. Ibid., 186.

A Final Note from Allison

An epidemic of major proportion is plaguing our nation today. This has become obvious to me as I travel the country sharing my God Allows U-Turns testimony and outreach. Seldom does a week go by when I'm not approached by people in deep pain concerning their adult child. Some come from my audience when I speak on this troubling issue, but others are fellow authors, speakers, and entertainers, some quite well-known, who are in the throes of familial discord concerning out-of-control adult children. It's happening all over the country to people from all walks of life.

During the years I spent as an enabling parent, no support groups were available for me as a parent in pain. I needed to hear from others who had walked in my shoes—I needed to hear what they were doing that was working. I needed people around me who would lovingly hold me accountable to my own choices as I experienced the journey of parenting and enabling a dysfunctional adult child. I needed an action plan to help me make changes in my life.

That's why, when I was writing *Setting Boundaries with Your Adult Children*, I knew beyond the shadow of a doubt that a vital part of the outreach would be the development of an international support group network based on the six SANITY steps I had developed.

We parents need a resource that can help us set appropriate boundaries and regain some SANITY in our households—and our lives. Your decision to read this book and to follow the steps I outline is a start in the right direction. And I believe the next vital step for you will be to regularly attend or help facilitate a SANITY support group in your community to help you gain hope as you walk the path to healing.

I encourage you to listen to your heart as you contemplate becoming involved in this growing outreach community. We need your help—parents and grandparents all over the country need your help.

Please consider joining us today in a network designed to strengthen our community. Here is how you can participate:

SANITY Support Group Network

- Offer support to other hurting parents.
- Become a group leader or facilitator.
- Help provide a meeting location.
- Become a faithful prayer warrior.
- Act as a virtual volunteer providing Internet assistance with an online newsletter, a blog, a chat room, communications, fundraising, and more at www.SettingBoundaries.com.

SANITY Community Forum

Join with fellow parents and grandparents around the country to gain support and encouragement in your journey to find SANITY. You are not alone! Visit our website to register for our FREE online Community Forum at www.SettingBoundaries.com.

SANITY Newsletter

In an effort to help empower our community of struggling parents and grandparents, we have developed a newsletter called *Setting Boundaries*. Each publication is distributed via e-mail and contains updates on SANITY support groups around the country, success stories, tips for parents, volunteer opportunities, profiles on board members, and other information vital to the outreach. Visit our web site www.SettingBoundaries.com to subscribe.

Our 12-Week Companion Study Guide

The first book in the acclaimed **Setting Boundaries** series is changing the lives of parents, grandparents, and entire communities around the world. Allison Bottke has developed the **SANITY Support Group Network** to work in tandem with the principles of **SANITY** outlined in the book. **SANITY Support Groups** are being conducted all around the country. The first **6-Steps to SANITY and 12-Weeks to Freedom** program specifically addresses the epidemic issue of enabling our adult children. The **Setting Boundaries Group Leader Start-up Kit** contains everything needed to equip and empower you to find freedom and **SANITY**. To locate or start a **SANITY Support Group** in your community, visit our website at www.SettingBoundaries.com.

LIVE Online Webcasts

Watch and listen to Allison LIVE in real time from the privacy of your home.

Online Support Groups

For those unable to attend a **SANITY Support Group** in your community, we offer online individual study.

For up-to-date information on all of the programs and products being offered by the **Setting Boundaries** outreach, sign up on our website today.

www.SettingBoundaries.com

About the Author

Allison Bottke is the general editor of the popular God Allows U-Turns series and the God Answers Prayer series and has written six books for children and youth, as well as contemporary fiction for baby-boomer women. Allison is in frequent demand as a speaker and has been featured on *The 700 Club, Decision Today,* and numerous other radio and television programs. Visit www.AllisonBottke.com.

HARVEST HOUSE
PUBLISHERS

Other Great Harvest House Reading

The Power of a Praying® Parent
By Stormie Ormartian

Stormie Omartian's mega best-selling The Power of a Praying® series (more than 8.2 million copies sold) is rereleased with fresh cover designs to reach those eager to discover the power of prayer in their lives. This resource will encourage readers in the parenting journey, whether their kids are 3 or 33.

When Your Teen Is Struggling: Real Hope and Practical Help for Parents Today
By Mark Gregston

Mark Gregston, founder of Heartlight Ministries, offers vital help to parents of teens who exhibit destructive or unhealthy behaviors and actions.

The Emotionally Destructive Relationship: Seeing It, Stopping It, Surviving It
By Leslie Vernick

Leslie Vernick, counselor and social worker, has witnessed the devastating effects of emotional abuse. Many, including many in the church, have not addressed this form of destruction in families and relationships because it is difficult to talk about. With godly guidance and practical experience. Vernick offers an empathetic approach to recognizing an emotionally destructive relationship and addresses the symptoms and damage with biblical tools.

The Mom I Want to Be: Rising Above Your Past to Give Your Kids a Great Future
By T. Suzanne Eller

A woman's experience as a mother is influenced by the mothering she received as a child. If neglect was a part of that upbringing, the woman who holds a newborn and faces the responsibility of parenting needs a healthy vision of motherhood. T. Suzanne Eller compassionately discusses how a woman can turn from a painful past and embrace a godly example of motherhood.

HARVEST HOUSE
PUBLISHERS

To learn more about Harvest House books
or to read sample chapters, log on to our Web site:

www.harvesthousepublishers.com

HARVEST HOUSE PUBLISHERS
EUGENE, OREGON